Praise for P9-BJR-266

In the past few years I've had the honor of watching Jeff Goins transition from a writer into a thought leader and one of the most exciting next generation voices. In this book, you'll see why and perhaps even more importantly how he did it.

Jon Acuff, New York Times bestselling author of **Start**

Jeff Goins has penned a beautiful reminder that time is sacred, of how even ordinary moments brim with heaven, and that great souls are forged in the crucible of delay. What a delight.

Ian Morgan Cron, bestselling author of **Jesus, My Father, the CIA, and Me: A Memoir . . . of Sorts** *and* **Chasing Francis: A Pilgrim's Tale**

If you find yourself in the quiet valley of waiting, Jeff Goins offers a kind voice in the silence. This gently honest book challenged me to surrender to the waiting moments rather than try to rush ahead to the next thing—a simply lovely read.

Emily P. Freeman, author of **A Million Little Ways** *and* **Grace for the Good Girl**

Jeff Goins is a master wordsmith. And this book is no exception. In it, he uses his personal journey and struggles to paint a poignant picture of what life could be like if you stopped rushing and started embracing each moment—even those seemingly long moments when you're stuck waiting for the next thing. Instead of living life wishing you could jump ahead to the next adventure, these pages will inspire you to slow down and savor the in-between.

Crystal Paine, founder of MoneySavingMom.com

According to Jeff Goins, life is more about waiting than we'd like. We try to avoid it at all costs. We linger over a past we can't repeat (or don't want to) or long for a future we can't reach. Either way we are not present to what is happening now. And that is precisely where the important stuff is happening. This book is a powerful reminder that we must embrace the "long game" of life, if we are to experience the love, joy, and peace we seek.

Michael Hyatt, New York Times bestselling author, former CEO of Thomas Nelson Publishers

The In-Between is a happy little reminder to stop hating the waiting, a lesson I've had to learn over and over again.

Myquillyn Smith, author of **The Nesting Place**

I distinctly remember, in second grade, thinking that my life would be perfect once I was a fifth grader—and so my thinking went until I was about 32. Needless to say, Jeff's book resounds clear to me, as a clarion call to live in the moment and make the most of life's waiting room moments. His storytelling is captivating and full of warmth and humor; this book is for anyone who loves to read stories about travel, wisdom, and redemption. I am thankful Jeff put into words the issue so many of us struggle with—how to be content when we live in-between.

Tsh Oxenreider, author and blogger at SimpleMom.net

Jeff Goins retells his life-so-far story, pointing out the treasures found along the way, and I'm suddenly more aware of the overlooked richness of my own life. Unflinchingly transparent, gentle, moving, smart and instructive but never preachy, *The In-Between* is a lesson in living deliberately with eyes wide open right where we are.

Shaun Groves, songwriter

For the adventurous heart, this book is a great reminder that some of the most exciting adventures happen right where you are. If you're anything like me, you feel bored sometimes by life, tired of waiting for the "next big thing," and a little too impatient to take things one day, one moment, at a time. The stories Jeff shares do a great job of reminding me to slow down and look around, because some of life's most important lessons, and best memories, happen while we're waiting.

Allison Vesterfelt, author of
Packing Light: Thoughts on Living Life with Less Baggage

I'm not good at waiting. I'm a traveler, I'm trying to get somewhere, and the "waiting" gets in my way. Then my friend Jeff emails me his new book, *The In-Between*. I began reading it on a flight in-between Tennessee and Texas, in-between one concert and the next, in-between busy and busier. Jeff has inspired me to see the value in what takes place in my life not only at point A and point B, but in the space where there doesn't seem to be a point. Jeff Goins wrote this book for me, and for anyone else who needs to embrace the waiting and exist in the in-between.

Warren Barfield, singer, songwriter, speaker

THE
In-Between

THE
In-Between

———

EMBRACING *the* TENSION BETWEEN
NOW *and the* NEXT BIG THING

———

JEFF GOINS

MOODY PUBLISHERS
CHICAGO

All Scripture quotations are taken from *The Holy Bible, English Standard Version*. Copyright © 2000, 2001 by Crossway Bibles, a division of Good News Publishers. Used by permission. All rights reserved.

Published in association with the literary agency of Mark Oestreicher.

Edited by Bailey Utecht
Interior design: Design Corps
Cover design: Kara Davison / Faceout Studio
Cover image: Shutterstock #34362736
Illustrations by: Mandy Thompson
Author Photo: Ashley Goins

Library of Congress Cataloging-in-Publication Data

Goins, Jeff.
   The in-between : embracing the tension between now and the next best thing / Jeff Goins.
      pages cm
   ISBN 978-0-8024-0724-5
   1. Life--Religious aspects—Christianity. 2. Christian life. 3. Change—Religious aspects—Christianity. 4. Expectation (Psychology)—Religious aspects—Christianity. 5. Waiting (Philosophy) I. Title.
   BV4501.3.G647 2013
   248.4—dc23

                          2013014296

Moody Publishers is committed to caring wisely for God's creation and uses recycled paper whenever possible. The paper in this book consists of 10 percent post-consumer waste.

We hope you enjoy this book from Moody Publishers. Our goal is to provide high-quality, thought-provoking books and products that connect truth to your real needs and challenges. For more information on other books and products written and produced from a biblical perspective, go to www.moodypublishers.com or write to:

Moody Publishers
820 N. LaSalle Boulevard
Chicago, IL 60610

1 3 5 7 9 10 8 6 4 2

Printed in the United States of America

For Aiden.
You're too young to know it now,
but someday you'll understand how much
you taught me before I ever started teaching you things.

Contents

Foreword

What we have is time. And what we do is waste it, waiting for those big spectacular moments. We think that something's about to happen—something enormous and newsworthy—but for most of us, it isn't. This is what I know: the big moments are the tiny moments. The breakthroughs are often silent, and they happen in the most unassuming of spaces.

Weddings are momentous, as are births, especially for moms. Beyond those two, though, most of the really significant and shaping moments of my life would be unrecognizable to anyone but me. That's how it is.

What I'm tempted to do right now is run you through story after story of how life can change in an instant—an accident, a disease undetected, violence. We know these stories. We hear them all the time. But if you're like me, sometimes you intentionally don't hear them. You absently stroke your kids' heads, you murmur a prayer, less a devout show of faith and more a whimper—*not us. Not us.*

And then you shake it off, square your shoulders, fasten your mind firmly elsewhere—details of the day: library books to return, oil to change and diapers, too.

You comfort yourself with the mindlessness of it, protecting yourself from the reality that your life is actually happening and you might not be there. It's scary to be there present, invested, right there on the front line of your life. It's easier to numb your-self with details and daily doings, waiting around for things to feel spectacular.

But this is it: this is as spectacular as it gets, and you have a choice, to be there or not.

I sat with an old friend today. She and her husband have en-dured unimaginable loss throughout the course of their lives, and another very fresh loss in these last months.

We sat in the golden fading light of a Chicago spring. Our kids ran around and around the screen porch, and the grass was impossibly green, almost glowing. And in the midst of all that wild and lush beauty, we sat facing one another, and she told me the particulars of that most recent loss. What I heard in her voice stunned me, moved me, instructed me.

She was present to it, unafraid. She told me about it unflinch-ingly, and what I realized is that she decided a long time ago that she wasn't waiting for perfect and she wasn't numbing herself against the worst case scenario. She had seen the worst case sce-nario, more times over than any of us should have to.

What I saw in her was a vision for how I want to live: in the midst of one her darkest seasons, twisted with uncertainty, bruised by the words of former friends, she sat with me, present and un-armed by busy-ness. She looked in my eyes and told me they'd be fine. She told me funny and sweet things about her kids, asked me about myself.

She wasn't waiting for the good part. She knows that these are the good parts, even while they're the bad parts. She wasn't shut down, going through the motions. She wasn't holding tight till this season passed. She was right there with me, right there with her kids, right in all the glory and pain and mess and beauty of a spring night in between everything.

That's how I want to be. That's who I want to be: deeply present in the present, in the mess, in the waiting, in the entirely imperfect right now.

That's what this book is about. Jeff has opened his life and his stories to us, and in doing that, he's written each one of us an invitation to the life that's actually passing before our eyes, whether or not we can see it. Jeff's rich and wise words are an invitation to what we may have dismissed as the warm-up, the throwaway moments.

But what my friend knows is that there are no throwaway moments—not when it's easy, not when it's hard, not when it's boring, not when you're waiting for something to happen. Throw those moments away at your own peril.

Throw those moments away and you will look back someday, bereft at what you missed, because it's the good stuff, the best stuff. It's all there is.

—**Shauna Niequist, author of** *Cold Tangerines,*
Bittersweet, **and** *Bread & Wine*

Introduction

LIFE BETWEEN *the* PANELS

How we spend our days, according to Annie Dillard, is how we spend our lives.[1] If that's true, then I spend most of my life waiting. Waiting in the checkout line at the grocery store. Waiting to rent a movie. Waiting for the movie to end. Waiting to turn thirty. Waiting for the weekend. Waiting for vacation.

Waiting, waiting, waiting.

Life is an endless series of appointments and phone calls and procrastinated tasks that need to, but sometimes never, get done. It's a long list of incomplete projects and broken promises that tomorrow will be better. It's being put on hold and waiting in office lobbies and watching that stupid hourglass rotate again and again on the computer screen. It's load times and legal processes—long, drawn-out bureaucratic systems that leave me sitting, watching the clock.

Life is one big wait.

Once an adventure seeker, my days are now full of responsibility. Gone are the days of hopping trains through Europe and trekking across the country in a van. Now, things have slowed down. As a dad, husband, and homeowner, I've got more than a few ings on my plate. But despite this busyness, most days feel fairly static, as if everything is standing still. And in this stillness, I'm learning to be present, to acknowledge the lessons life is trying to teach me. Because even in an adventure, you have to wait, to deal with what happens when things don't turn out the way you expect.

Between raising a child and learning to be a better spouse, all while managing the challenges of working from home and starting a business with less time than before, I'm feeling the tension between how I used to live and what's reality. My schedule is full of obligations and opportunities that tempt me to push through the *now*, moving on to the next thing. I'm tempted with distractions, to linger in the glory of the past or hold out hope for a better future. These are all ways I distance myself from the moment. And I wonder why the abundant life I've been searching for seems so evasive, even taunting at times.

In frustration, I'm confronted with an old lesson of letting go, of looking beyond personal ambition and replacing it with something better. The slow growth that happens when I surrender to what life—and maybe God—is trying to teach me. So it seems, despite a penchant for travel, that the antidote to my restlessness is not another trip or adventure, but a deep abiding in where I am right now. How does this happen? With waiting. Normal, everyday situations that test my patience and cause me to reflect on what really matters. I don't like it, but I'm starting to see the value of the times in between the big moments in life.

I've spent my whole life longing for the next season, hoping better things would come when I graduated or got married or gave my life to a career worthy of my talents. But now I'm not sure holding out for what's to come is the smartest strategy. And I have a feeling that I'm not alone.

We all want to live meaningful lives full of experiences we can be proud of. We all want a great story to tell our grandchildren. But many of us fail to recognize that the best moments are the ones happening right now.

Maybe the "good stuff" isn't ahead of or behind us. Maybe it's somewhere in between. Right in the midst of this moment, here and now. Maybe Annie Dillard is right. Maybe what we call "mundane," what feels boring and ordinary, is really how we spend our lives. And we have an opportunity to make of it what we will—to resent its lack of adventure or rejoice in its beauty. Perhaps, the abundant life we've been seeking has little to do with big events and comes in a subtler form: embracing the pauses in between major beats.

WHAT I DIDN'T LEARN FROM COMIC BOOKS

When I was a teenager, I read comic books. First, Superman, then Spiderman; then more sophisticated story lines like Batman and X-Men and even later, Spawn and The Maxx. On my weekly Saturday trip to the comic store, I spent what little money was left in my wallet on these short stories, and then I would rush home to read them. They always ended before I wanted, no matter how hard I tried to drag them out, looking at each panel intently.

Short and exciting, comic books led me to believe that life is supposed to be this way, too. As an adolescent, I imagined how great it would be to live such a story, craving the excitement contained on each page and longing for that same sense of adventure in my own life. But as I've grown up and have started to see the slowness of life, I've had a crisis of faith in my own story. Is it inevitable that our experiences tend toward the more mundane as we mature, or is there an opportunity here?

r or two ago, my wife took me to the Belcourt Theatre
lle to see a film about comic books. Titled *Super*, the film
was about a guy who's read one too many comics and decides to
stand up to injustice. I didn't particularly enjoy the movie, but one
scene eloquently expressed this idea of waiting and how it fits in
with the rest of life.

In the scene, the main character, Frank, who runs around
town killing bad guys with an oversized monkey wrench, is sitting
with his self-appointed teenage sidekick, Libby. They're waiting
for an opportunity to fight evil, for the police sirens to blare or
something significant to happen. But nothing does. So they sit in
boredom, wondering what they should do.

Frank: *Maybe you need to be bored sometimes.*
Libby: *You don't see them bored in comic books.*
Frank: *That's what happens in between the panels.*
Libby: *Wow, in between the panels! Is that where we are right now?*[2]

As I watched the scene unfold on the screen, I thought: *Yes, this
is where we spend our lives—in between the panels.*
We all want a life we can be proud of, one that looks a little
more like the stories we read in books or watch on the big screen.
But real life doesn't happen like that. It doesn't feel like an adventure most of the time; in fact, it can seem rather boring. And as
hard as we try to make it so, we are still occasionally stuck with
less-than-remarkable moments. So what do we do with those?

Here's the good news: this is not the end of the tale. We are not
condemned to lives of insignificance and mediocrity. But life does
slow down, inconveniences do occur, and delays happen to the
best of us. The challenge is what we do with these times, how we

use — or waste — our waiting. The slower times contain a wealth of wisdom for us to tap into, but only when we recognize them.

Otherwise we grow detached, disillusioned. Embittered toward the disappointments of life, we begin to believe there's nothing more to existence than endless tasks and chores. That's why so many of us fight the quiet and try to fill the void with constant activity. It's why we sometimes stay up late at night, wondering if satisfaction is ever attainable. All the while, we miss the truth: the thing we want to escape is what holds the key to our contentment.

What if, instead of pining for the action of the next frame, we surrendered to the wait, learning to live in those "boring" moments with more intentionality? What if we fell in love with the in-between times, relishing instead of resenting them? Well then, we might just learn a few important lessons.

WE LEARN TO SLOW DOWN

In a world saturated with social media and unlimited interruptions, many of us struggle to focus on what's in front of us. With so many voices vying for our attention — billboard ads and TV commercials and annoying Internet pop-ups — it's hard to know what's worth our attention. We end up tuning it all out, the good with the bad.

The surprising solution to our distraction confronts us every day. At the shopping mall. In long lines of traffic. Even standing at the coffeepot. Every time we wait is an opportunity to slow down and be present in an increasingly noisy world, to listen to the voices we sometimes lose in the static.

And as we embrace the wait, we learn to appreciate the delays and postponements that teach us some things in life are worth waiting for.

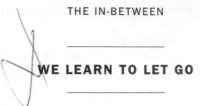

WE LEARN TO LET GO

Life was meant to be more than the daily humdrum. It was supposed to be enjoyable, full of purpose, not just stress and worry. So where has all our satisfaction gone? Where is our pleasure, our joy? We search on road trips and vacations for the life we've always wanted. We seek out meaning in our jobs. We even reserve those feelings of joy and satisfaction for major events like marriage or the birth of a child. But often we're disappointed with what we find. Sure, we may be happy; but we are far from complete. Even the best job, best husband, and best vacation have their flaws.

What we were hoping for, what we dreamed would be a larger-than-life experience, ends up looking a lot like morning breath and spreadsheets. So we keep searching, and we wonder why it's becoming harder to sit still and just *be*. All the while, what we're searching for sits in front of us, hidden in normal, everyday inconveniences.

If we reserve our joy only for the experiences of a lifetime, we may miss the life in the experience. Such opportunities are everywhere, waiting for us to see them. But first we must learn to open our eyes, to recognize the gift of waiting.

WE LEARN TO BE GRATEFUL

In the in-between, we learn to recognize the temporal nature of life, and that eventually all waiting must end. When it does, we are left with what we did with the time in between the beginning and the end.

Watching a tree grow will likely drive you crazy. It's a process if you stand there, impatiently tapping your foot, for it to *do* something. But if you step away and come back later, you'll be surprised to see something beautiful emerge. The fact is the plant *is* doing something: it's growing. Just not as quickly as you might like. Our culture has conditioned us to expect instant results and overnight success; this impatience runs so rampant that we dress it up in terms like "efficiency" and "productivity." But really what's happening is we are conditioning ourselves to get what we want now, all the time. This mindset robs us of the lessons that waiting can teach us, causing us to miss out on the slow but important stuff of life.

Most growth happens this way: slowly, over time. You don't see it happening—in fact, sometimes the circumstances feel more like inconveniences than opportunities—but then one day you wake up, amazed at how far you've come. When it comes to waiting, we have a choice. We can try to bypass the delays to get immediate gratification. Or we can embrace the "long game" of life and invest those days, months, and years in the slow but intentional growth that leads to lasting change.

In this book, I'm going to share how I've learned those lessons in different seasons of my own life. But as you read, my hope is you think of your own experiences and the lessons life was trying to teach you, and is teaching you right now.

Together, we're going to explore what happens when we realize the dull moments are the ones shaping us into who we're supposed to be. Maybe you'll recall a few times that forced you to wait and how that discomfort caused you to grow, to learn to be content with not being finished. Maybe you'll even learn, as I did, that we can sit by and watch life pass us, or we can choose to participate in it, even the slow parts—especially, the slow parts.

A FINAL THOUGHT (OR PERHAPS, A WARNING)

All the stories in this book actually happened, but not every person I've talked to agrees with *how* they happened. I've done my diligence in asking those who were present if they remembered things as I did. At times, we agreed; at others, we did not. And sometimes, none of us was sure about exactly what happened. And I think that's okay. Nobody's memory is perfect, and when mine failed me, I did my best to fill in the blanks with dialogue and detail of what likely happened. A book like this isn't supposed to be just a recounting of history; it's an exploration of what I remember and how it changed me. And I hope it changes you too, at least in some small way.

So let's journey through the in-between together.

part one

SLOW DOWN

My earliest memory is of a waiting room. I must be really young—no more than three or four years old—because I'm playing on the floor with a few books and toys. The scene is so vague that I wonder if maybe it was only a dream that I'm now appropriating as memory. My mom is at the dentist's office, having some work done on her teeth, and I am with her. Fiddling around with whatever I can find, I pick up a book and stare at the words, too young to read; I flip through a *Highlights* magazine; I play with toys and bide my time. I wait.

Mom is gone maybe ten minutes, but it feels like two hours.

The memory is neither sweet nor sour; it just is. And maybe that's the significance: this is my earliest memory, maybe God's way of saying what the rest of life will look like.

We spend our lives waiting. We wait in line, wait to graduate, wait for our family to get a clue. We may even eagerly wait for "the one," to fall in love and run away with the person we were made for.

While we are young, we long for freedoms that haven't come: the ability to drive ourselves to work without mom or dad in the passenger's seat, the chance to move away and see the world, the opportunity to vote or sign that first apartment lease. We wait to be who we are, to receive permission to live our lives. And then, we wait for job promotions and test results and for our kids to phone home from college. We search and wander, looking for a place to land. And as we do this, we may miss an opportunity to live right now, to slow down.

We miss the moment.

Some of the most trying times to wait are the ones we don't anticipate: not an impending marriage or a baby about to be born, but a time when our ideals are not met, when our aspirations are delayed, when life doesn't happen as we'd like. Those are the times we grow.

Waiting is the great grace. It's a subtle sign for those with eyes to see, reminding us there is work yet to be done—not just around us, but in us. We are still in progress, unfinished masterpieces full of incompletion. And although I know this, I resist it. For the fruit of waiting—the outcome, the resulting growth—I am grateful. But for the process—the part that causes the growth—I am not. Waiting is hard. It forces us to acknowledge our imperfections, our own unfinishedness. It is the long ride home; the journey, not the destination. We see the shore but have not arrived. This is why we hate to wait, why we feel taunted by these delays and slow-downs. They force us to rely patience and faith to fill the gap between where we are and want to be.

I'm terrible at waiting, simply awful at it. Just this morning, I opened my laptop to check email, and as my messages began to download, I opened a web browser. While that loaded, I checked Twitter on my phone. Incapable of wasting a single second, to simply sit still and soak in my surroundings, I must always do something. I must squeeze the most out of every moment, unaware that this leaves little left to savor.

I blame TV for what it's done to my brain, the Internet for how it's made me impatient. But the truth is, I'm the one who chooses to be restless, the one who gives in to temptations to find the next thrill, while refusing the joy of what's in front of me.

However, it seems I am not the only one who does this. Many of us are speeding up and skipping over, missing tho *important* as we scan for the *urgent*. The irony is that in our anxiety toward not missing out, we are losing the most meaningful moments of life.

The other day, I went outside to sit on my back porch, leaving my phone in the house. As I rocked my son to sleep, I looked to my left and saw a huge cumulus cloud growing in the sky. Every second as I watched, it grew, marshmallowing into a great, big cotton ball in the sky. My first inclination was to run inside, grab my phone, and snap a photo. To capture the memory and share it with friends. But some internal urge prevented me from doing so. Resisting the compulsion to capture the moment, I instead chose a different route: to appreciate it. Sitting there and allowing the scene to take me, I knew there was something sacred in that moment, something special and important about being there.

Call me arrogant, but that cloud came out of hiding just for me. It lasted only a minute and then passed, fading away forever into the oblivion of blue. And I nearly missed it.

A minute later, my wife called from the kitchen, asking me to come inside.

Everything important in life is like this—here one moment and gone the next. All we have are these moments, and what we choose to do with them is what we choose to do with our lives. We can miss or relish every one.

Something gets lost when we rush from one moment to the next, when we try to squeeze too much out of the times we're supposed to wait. Something is sacrificed when we race through the valley to get to the mountaintop, when we hurry past those in need on our way to the next appointment.

We were made to wait, to long for things unseen. This is the place from which dreams and desires come. It's a place of trust—and we find it not in the resolution, but the incompletion. If you've ever stood in line to get your driver's license or waited outside the Apple store, you know what I'm talking about. We don't love the process, but the results are worth the striving.

What we fail to notice as we stand in line—as we wait—is that we, ourselves, are changing. We're growing and adapting to what's around us, maybe even becoming someone new. At least, we can be. We have the opportunity. Whether we take it or not is up to us.

All this waiting is not an accident; it's a call to slow down. These delays are meant to point us to a deeper truth: we are not finished. If we relish this reality and embrace the opportunity it holds, we may be able to grasp a depth we've not yet reached. We may find this abundant life, after all.

The good life comes like most good things—unexpectedly—in moments that are fading away faster than we realize. These are the moments that take our time but don't demand our attention. When we miss them, they're gone. In those times especially, we would do well to slow down and be present, because we won't get them back.

CHAPTER ONE
Siestas

SEARCHING *for a* BREAKTHROUGH

One foot off the plane in Madrid and assaulted by a cloud of cigarette smoke, I knew things were going to be different. In the States, people didn't stand in circles arbitrarily dubbed "smoking zones" and exhale carbon monoxide in innocent strangers' faces. Coughing while I passed such a circle, it dawned on me that I was going to be learning a lot more than Spanish that semester.

A two-hour layover, then we were on to our final destination: Seville.

After arriving in the city with fifty travel companions, I boarded a charter bus full of fellow wide-eyed American college students. As we drove around, gawking at palm trees and olive-skinned commuters, we migrated to our host homes.

Dropped off two-by-two, we settled into the places where we'd be living.

Upon arriving at Asturias Street, the bus was half empty. My heart beginning to thump, I readied myself to meet the people who would be my family for the next three and a half months.

Greeted at the door by a smiling four-foot-something woman, I felt warm lips pressed against both cheeks. My ears were overwhelmed by phrases I barely discerned to be Spanish. Her name was Loli, and she spoke so quickly and with such a thick accent that five and a half years of studying the language were instantly rendered useless.

Crossing cultures should have been easy. Having spent the previous summer in Texas away from my native Illinois, I figured an overseas jaunt would be a piece of cake. How different could another few months in a foreign place be? But despite the similarities in weather, Spain was no Texas. So far, nobody spoke a lick of English, and the people were far less friendly than those in the Southwestern United States.

A few months before going to Europe, my friend Dustin and I hopped into his Chevy pickup to drive sixteen hours from Springfield, Illinois, to Austin, Texas. That first night at the camp we'd be working at for the summer, we slept outside beneath the stars. That summer was full of adventure: we got into the best shape of our lives, grew out our hair, and learned to seize every day for what it had to offer. Dustin started swimming, and I fell in love with running. We were both obsessed with doing as much as we could so we would later have great stories to tell. Racing from one event to the next, never bothering to catch our breath or ask for directions, we refused to miss a thing.

I thought my time in Spain would be similar to my summer in Texas.

I was wrong.

My roommate, Daniel, arrived at Loli's home the day after I did. At first, Daniel and I didn't talk. Unlike my fast-paced summer camp mindset, he had a slower philosophy of life. Having grown up in Idaho, he spent his free time relaxing—and snowboarding. Maybe it was his upbringing or personality, but Daniel didn't seem to be bothered by much. Nothing ever stressed him out or caused him to rush. And frankly, this bugged me. I was in a hurry to do *everything*: to travel the world, meet new people, and begin my adventure. After we said our pleasantries, my roommate and I fell into our respective routines, which had little to do with each other.

A group of students from my study abroad program investigated some exchange opportunities that allowed us to teach Spaniards English while we learned Spanish from them. The practice was great, but the point was to build real relationships, to make lasting connections with locals. Simply learning and living in another city wasn't enough for me; I wanted more. It was a pride issue. I wanted an impressive story to tell, something more ~ the typical "I went to Spain, and all I got was this lousy T-shirt."

Halfway through the semester, one of the guys in our program started dating a Spanish woman, and that made me jealous. Not because I wanted to date her, but because I wanted the story. A Spanish girlfriend? Can you imagine what people would say? Back home, I had a girlfriend, but she was just an ordinary American girl. Her skin was slightly tanner than my pasty variety, but she didn't speak any foreign language fluently. And I was pretty sure she wasn't of gypsy descent—which equated to "boring" in my book. Truthfully, my girlfriend was prettier than my friend's Mediterranean beauty, but that didn't matter. What mattered was he'd done something nobody else did. And it drove me nuts.

I had to find a better story.

Packing my schedule with every activity I could find, I attended church events, frequented flamenco bars, and connected with university students for free language lessons.

Mornings in Spain ran on routine. Getting up around seven, I would jump into the shower to quickly bathe myself before the hot water ran out. Next was Daniel, who always maximized his sleeping time and took his time with everything else. Then, we'd arrive at the breakfast table only before we needed to rush out the door for school. In typical college-student fashion, we often procrastinated, trying to fit as much as we could into as little time as possible.

No matter when we sat down for breakfast, we'd always find Loli already there. It didn't matter how hurried we seemed, she always took her time. Each morning, she'd greet us with a smile and hot plate full of food, telling us to take our time as we scarfed down our toast. You have to understand something: Spanish *tostado* is nothing like a slice of crusty American carbohydrates pulled from a plastic bag and burnt beyond freshness. *Tostado*—at least in Loli's house—was a huge hunk of freshly baked bread, lightly toasted to perfection and smothered with whole-fruit *mermelada* that made store-bought jams and jellies back home seem flavorless. It took minutes just to apply the spread. Despite the deliciousness of the experience, I always tried to rush it.

When we finished eating, Loli would pull out a small Bible study booklet that Daniel and I took turns reading from every morning. Even when were in a hurry, she insisted on our spiritual nourishment before beginning our busy days. As sweet as this was, I initially found it frustrating. Didn't she understand we had somewhere to be? Or at least, I did. Instead of bustling around to accommodate our hurry, Loli would simply sit still, waiting as we gobbled our toast and gulped our juice. Then she'd ask one of us to read.

When it was Daniel's turn, we were in trouble. He joined the program with no previous education in Spanish, so it took him a long time to stumble through a five-hundred-word religious reading in a nonnative tongue. As my terrible luck would have it, those were the days we were running the latest.

After finishing the reading, we'd both spring out the door, jogging part of the mile-long jaunt to school.

The first part of the semester was full of frustration at moments that took longer than they "should" have. At Loli for holding us up. At Daniel for not knowing Spanish. At an entire culture for taking so much time to do, well, everything. For months, I blamed others for making me wait, for not conforming to my expectations. But eventually, I began to see the opportunity this afforded me.

About a month into the semester, Loli asked if I wanted to go on a church retreat with her. Daniel and I had been attending the church where Loli's older son, Juan, was the preacher. Each week, we left exhausted by the long services and hard-to-follow preaching. Learning Spanish in Seville was like learning English in the Deep South of the US: accents are thick and loose, and slang runs rampant. For a textbook learner, following a Spanish-speaking preacher from Seville can be confusing, if not completely disorienting. Despite this, I decided to go on the retreat. *It'll be good for me*, I thought, *to get out of the city and see a slower side of life.*

At the time, I'd been going out nearly every night for the past three weeks, staying up till three in the morning, sleeping a few hours, and then getting up for school the next morning only to doze off in class. It had started to wear on me. Maybe this retreat would be just that: a chance to recoil from my self-imposed busy-ness and reboot. I hoped so.

The weekend began as expected: long services with passionate preaching that sent me straight to sleep. I wanted to follow along, but regardless of how hard I tried, I couldn't keep up. Which is why this was the weekend I began drinking coffee. Never having the stomach for it, I was desperate for something to keep me awake during the drawn-out prayers and extended worship times. I had no choice.

Scooping a few heaps of *Cola Cao* into my espresso, I took my first sip of the drink and winced. Too strong. A few more scoops of the cocoa drink, add some more milk, and *there*—it tasted nothing like coffee. Perfect. I guzzled down the caffeinated beverage as if it were the elixir of life. And to me, it was. By the end of the week-end, I was a full-fledged *café con leche* addict.

Despite the coffee in my system, I still found the services hard to follow. The preacher, who was a guest of the church, spoke quickly and excitedly—so much that I couldn't keep track of whether we were talking about Moses or John the Baptist. The vocabulary words and expressions he was using confused me even further. As I flipped through my dictionary in a fury and failing to find the word before he was on to another subject, I decided it was no use. He might as well have been speaking Yiddish.

In between services, I stepped outside for a breath of fresh air. *Going for a walk will do me some good.* Circling around the retreat center, I prayed for a miracle. I started to feel it was a mistake to have come here. Maybe to have come to Spain at all. As I thought this, a voice called out to me. For a second, I thought it was the Almighty calling back in response to my prayer. But then I heard it clearer the second time; it was a child's voice.

"*Pepe!*" came the voice from behind one of the brick buildings of which there was an abundance here.

A young boy appeared from behind the building and walked toward me.

"*Soy Pablo,*" he said.

Ah, yes. The pastor's kid. As he approached, Pablo grabbed my hand and tugged at it. Curious, I let him lead me to a small, hut-like concrete house where he and the other children were playing.

Pablo introduced me to the group—there were six or seven of them, all gathered together. He pushed me to the front of the group and scooted a lectern in front of me. Yes, a lectern. And then he said the most bizarre thing I thought a kid could say: "*Predica.*"

Preach.

As in, deliver a sermon. A message. A homily.

My jaw dropped. This was a joke, right? But it wasn't. The kids, as if on cue, all took a seat, their eyes fixed on me, some with Bibles open in their laps.

This is their idea of fun? Doing a pretend church service? I secretly wondered if this might be a cult.

But when I realized they weren't going to let me go u
heard some kind of message, I did what they asked: I preac....
In Spanish, with my bilingual Bible open to help me cheat, I did
the best I could, improvising in places when possible. It wasn't elo-
quent, but the kids didn't mind, nor did they notice I was plagia-
rizing the entire commentary section from my Spanish New Tes-
tament. Throughout the course of my "message," the little ones
occasionally emitted tiny "Amens" and spontaneously erupted in
worshipful applause. "Alleluia!" one said when I stumbled over a
word that was hard to pronounce.

The sermon concluded, and they all stood in unison to sing a
song. Not knowing the words, I joined them, anyway. Their passion was contagious. They piously passed an offering plate and
even dropped a few euro coins into it.

As the service came to an end, I glanced around, watching
these kids emulate what they'd seen their parents do a thousand
times.

Maybe, I thought, *they aren't pretending at all.*

At the end of the service, a little girl, not quite nine years old,
approached me with her hand extended. Confused, I shook it.

"*Gracias, pastor,*" she said. *Thank you, pastor.* But it was more than
gratitude; it was a reminder. Literally, the word can be translated,
"graces." Watching the little ones linger in this ramshackle sanctu-
ary, shaking each other's hands, I smiled—struck by the beauty of
the moment. After a month of trying not to fall asleep on Sunday
mornings, I'd finally found a church service I could connect with.
"Let the little children come to me," Jesus told the religious leaders
(Matthew 19:14). Indeed, they did come, and they were generous
enough to bring me along with them.

After the retreat, I returned to the city and to my routine—but
not as it once was. The fast pace of life I'd been experiencing

began to feel empty. Of course, the experiences were the same, but I was different.

One evening, though, everything started to slow down.

On my way to meet some friends, I met a man named Micah. A beggar and a drifter, he was from Germany and had run into some hard luck. Having lost his immigration papers, Micah was unable to find work. He needed help. But I was busy and had plans.

After ignoring and then flat-out refusing him, I walked away, trying to create some distance between myself and the man. Getting only about a hundred yards away, I heard a voice tell me to turn around, to stop rushing and running and give in to the mystery of the moment — regardless of how busy I thought I was.

Or maybe it was Micah's voice, screaming, "For the love of Jesus Christ, help me!" That could have been what made me turn around, too.

I took Micah to McDonald's, where he told me his story. He came to Spain in search of work, but after losing his papers, his life became hard. He'd been living on the streets for years now, unable to return to his native Germany and unable to find work in Seville. He was stuck.

For an hour, Micah and I got to know each other. Hearing his story of how he ended up on the streets, I began to care, to actually listen. And then he told me something I'd never considered — and would never forget.

"You are the only one." The only one? The only one to what? Listen? Buy him a meal?

"What do you mean?" I asked.

"To stop," he said, pausing to lift a handful of fries to his mouth. "I've been standing on that street corner for months. And you were the only one who stopped. . . . Why?"

I swallowed hard, unsure of how to explain myself.

"Well," I said. "I guess . . . it's because of what you said ___ Jesus. I believe in Him, and I think it's what He'd want me to do. To stop and help you, I mean." I hung my head in shame. What a pitiful theological explanation.

Micah glared at me for a moment, as if suspicious of what I was saying, and I didn't blame him. I thought it sounded crazy, too. Then he cracked a small smile, which slowly grew into a full grin. And he plunged another handful of fries into his mouth, saying, "I love God."

And that was it.

Walking home that night, I couldn't stop smiling, recalling that pre-fry-plunge face. Later, I wrote in my journal that I'd never felt so alive. The next day, I asked Loli to pack an extra sandwich for me. I no longer avoided interruptions; I planned for them.

But making connections with strangers was difficult. As the semester went on, I became even busier, which made it hard to do those things that had made my experience stand out. What's more, Spanish people did not seem to keep appointments as well as Americans — another complication that made it difficult to pack as much activity as possible into a few short months.

This was part of my problem. I was always moving on to another experience, never patient enough to stick with my current commitments and instead, rushing on to the next thing. But in Spain, this was hard to do.

Sevillians aren't quite so concerned with punctuality. They have a phrase — *no pasa nada* — which literally means, "nothing happens." It's similar to the American phrase, "no big deal." Late for a meeting? *No pasa nada.* Need to skip class today to take care of a personal issue? *No pasa nada.* Such a cultural mindset was freeing; and the more of it I experienced, the more I wanted. And although it took months of rebellion before I could succumb to this laid-back way of life, that little expression eventually saved me. There was a power to the words that transcended shame, a potency in embracing the unexpected. That simple, carefree phrase taught me to let go of my little plans in exchange for a bigger picture. It meant being able to laugh at myself at times and accept when things didn't turn out the way I'd hoped. That semester was full of *no pasa nada* moments in which I was stirred awake, realizing I was rushing when I should have been resting.

One night after supper, I did something different: I stayed home. Sitting with Loli in the living room where the TV provided the after-dinner entertainment, I didn't do my normal evening custom. Instead of excusing myself and heading out for the night, I stayed put. Every night, Loli did this; she sat in front of the television, often accompanied by Daniel. This always baffled me. Why wouldn't he join me in taking advantage of every moment we had here? It seemed lazy, like he was squandering a great opportunity. But night after night of going out had worn me down to exhaustion. Anything, I guess—even flamenco clubs in Seville—can start to feel old. The sense of adventure had faded, and I was searching again for what was really missing.

Daniel, Loli, and I watched TV that night. And we laughed for hours. When Loli would laugh hysterically at something we didn't quite understand, we'd fake a few chuckles, anyway. The moment was entirely mundane, but nonetheless magical.

Around midnight, we said good night and went to bed. And that was all there was to it. No stunning breakthroughs or grand experiences. Just a night with the woman who made our meals and loved us better than we deserved. I had traveled across the Atlantic Ocean to run away from the ordinariness of life, to find an adventure. I never expected much from my host family; they were just the launching pad for my adventurous exploits.

But in my striving to feed homeless people and build cultural relationships and take on the nightlife of Seville, I found myself tired. A life filled with movement, with constant motion and no rest stops, isn't a life at all. It's tourism. Life's mundane moments—ordinary times of TV-watching and breakfast-eating—can be embraced as a slow, deliberate, beautiful way of life if we pay attention and see what's really there.

After that night, I gave up on the constant outings, weekends away, and began to look for a simpler, slower kind of life. I found it at "home" with Loli, around the dinner table and the TV. I started going to bed earlier, waking up at a decent hour, and getting to the table before she did. Instead of rushing through a delicious meal, I took my time with the toast. The breakfast and Bible study and moments of conversation before the day started were simple graces, gentle reminders that I was going too fast. I finally stopped fighting them and took my time, allowing myself to enjoy the simple events preceding my big plans for the day.

Soon, I learned that few other students in our program ate freshly baked bread for breakfast each morning, and that nobody's *señora* sat around waiting to read the Bible with them. I was lucky and didn't even know it. That's often the case with busyness: it robs us of the gifts right in front of us.

As these changes began to take place, I found myself changing, too. Each morning, I would try to beat Daniel to be the first to volunteer to read from Loli's Bible study booklet. Instead of avoiding this chance to practice my Spanish, I embraced it. Not to mention, it made my host mom happy.

After class, we'd return home around half past three for lunch, the biggest meal of the day. At the end of the meal, Loli would ask, "*Postre?*" which is Spanish for "Dessert?" And we would always shrug, feigning indifference. Then she'd smile knowingly and list what she had, which usually included some fresh fruit, yogurt, and the Spanish dessert staple: *flan*. We always chose flan—so much that this became a running joke. Daniel and I would pretend to sincerely struggle over what we wanted for dessert each day and then consent to flan. Loli eventually wised up and stopped buying yogurt and fruit and, well, anything but lots and lots of flan.

In my mind, there is a clear distinction between what Spain was like before that night of TV-watching with Loli and what it was like after. Although I went out less for the second half of the semester, I still enjoyed a few big events, including some travel to places like Portugal and Italy. And it was in Italy where I once again heard the call to slow down and appreciate what was in front of me.

———

Later in the semester, I was traveling with a few friends for vacation. We set out to see it all. First, France: a midnight stop in Nice. Then an afternoon cappuccino in Genoa before arriving in Rome. We stood in the mile-long line to see the Vatican, reenacted scenes from *Gladiator* outside the Colosseum, and visited just about every gelato joint we could find. But by the third day, we were wiped, completely exhausted.

One afternoon, we decided to take a nap. Just a short one, we told ourselves. We had been running so hard, we thought it was the least we deserved. So we retreated to our hostel, took showers, set an alarm clock, and went to bed. The next thing we knew, we awoke, well rested and ready to spend the rest of the day sightseeing. There was just one problem: it was dark outside! We had overslept by four hours, wasting our afternoon and snoozing well into the evening. After an epic-length nap, we'd be lucky to find a restaurant still serving supper. But the funny thing was, we weren't mad; we laughed about the experience. Why were we trying so hard? What was there to prove? Were we just trying to impress our friends, to fill up our photo albums? After that, we gave up on seeing everything. Instead of adding blips to a radar screen of tourist checkpoints, we decided to create a few lasting memories.

One afternoon, Dustin and I borrowed a couple of guitars from some street musicians and performed Van Morrison's "Brown Eyed Girl" for a crowd of a hundred. Another time, we ended up on *Piazza Grande*, an Italian TV game show, in front of three million daytime viewers.

But nothing would compare to what we found in Florence.

We spent three days in Rome and then another three in Florence, home of the Renaissance. Our stay there was much different from Rome: We started out with the intention of taking it slow and embracing opportunities to wait. We bought leather goods, took our time eating pizza and pasta, and Dustin even got a date with an Italian woman. After a couple days of doing nothing particularly touristy, we decided to see *David*, Michelangelo's most famous sculpture. It was such an iconic piece; we had to go. Having spent most of the day on our feet, we arrived at the Accademia Gallery, the museum that holds *David*. We joined an endless conga line of tourists, all pushing their way forward to see the monolith. My three friends and I removed ourselves from the line and stood in the back of the room, then we gradually grew tired of standing and sank to the cold stone floor. As crowds came and left, we just sat, staring at the larger-than-life statue of the man who killed the giant.

Sitting and staring in awestruck silence, we beheld *David*. The details were so intricate; the more you looked at it, the more you saw. Piercing eyes and looping curls created movement and texture out of the same marble that formed arm muscles, tendons, even veins running over the backs of the man's hands and knuckles.

I'm not an art critic, but I recognize beauty when I see it. And this was beauty.

As people continued to trudge down the hall, entering and leaving the room, we stayed to soak in the view. There were other notable pieces to see, but we refused to leave that room for over three hours. Like many others, we had rushed past other works of art to see this one piece. And frankly, at first we had been ready to rush up close, check it out, and head right back out—until we stepped out of the fidgety long line and stopped for a moment. Until we sat down and noticed the beauty that others were missing. Until we waited.

None of us discussed whether or not to stay; we just sat down, as if immobilized. Other than the occasional whispered observation, not many words were spoken. Hours later, without cue we stood up and looked at each other and left. No one said a thing until we went to lunch, and the first word to escape any of our mouths was "Wow."

In Florence, we finally understood the lesson we had only flirted with in Rome. When we began our trip, we were obsessed with *more*—more sights, more experiences, more stories. But now we realized *more* wasn't better. Slower was better—fewer thrills, less hype, more memories.

I've come to realize I want to live a life like that. One that takes time to notice the things that other people are overlooking. One that slows down to sit and soak up the beauty. One that creates space for the "wow" moments. I want the kind of life that makes room for the art in all our lives. As Charles Whiston writes:

> No passing and hurried glance at a great painting as we stroll down the corridors of an art gallery will ever suffice to reveal to us its richness and significance. If we sit down in a quiet gallery and limit our attention to a single picture, then it will act upon us. For a great painting is an active agent and can affect us. We

need therefore to sit receptive, open-minded, alert, quiet, before it. Furthermore, no single introspection is sufficient. Many repeated visits to the same painting are required before we begin to grasp its significance. We know that we must wait patiently until, in its own way and time, it discloses its meanings. The truth in the painting must find and fit the need that is in us.[3]

The statue captivated and continued to teach us long after we saw it. *David* taught us to slow down, to do less, and to pay attention to the intricacies—the art—all around us. And we almost missed that moment, almost rushed right past the statue on our way to the next thing on our schedule. But instead, we sacrificed the opportunity to do more and decided to focus, to be present in the moment. And as a result, we had a "wow" moment.

"Hurry up and wait," said the man in the customs line behind me at the airport. We were in Detroit, the first of a few stops during this long travel day. It was December, and we fifty students were now headed home for Christmas. After months of learning and longing, of getting frustrated and growing, I was returning home. Back to the States. Back to Illinois cornfields. Back to bonfires and snow-covered highways and a girlfriend I'd grown apart from.

Catching a glimpse of myself in a piece of reflective glass, I barely recognized the person I saw. He was wearing slacks and a sweater; he had long sideburns and short hair and carried a brown, leather satchel. He looked, frankly, a little European.

As the months after studying abroad went by, I realized how much I'd changed. I would never be able to choke down gas station cappuccino again. I would correct my Spanish professor's grammar. I would look with derision on any piece of architecture less than five hundred years old. Those were the surface things, though. Most of all, I'd take time in the moments that I would normally rush through.

I relish the big stories from Europe—those major moments—but the memories that remain fixed in my mind are the small ones. The daily walk home from class with Daniel. Sermons with six-year-olds. Late nights of laughing with Loli. Taking in the beauty of a statue. Quiet mornings of reading. And of course, the flan.

In music, this type of passing moment has a name: a grace note. And that's just what these moments of waiting and walking and wondering were: grace notes that added a touch of beauty to the bolder moments making up the music of my days.

Hurry up and wait, indeed.

IN-BETWEEN GLIMPSES

I used to push it to the last minute every morning— calculating how long my routine took to the minute. Then I had three kids. Soon I realized there was no calculating anything. As my children became toddlers, I would get that retched impatient feeling like I was about to explode trying to rush them through simple things like getting dressed and tying their shoes. The mornings would be full of stress and yelling. I felt like a horrible mom.

So one day I woke up an hour early and decided no matter what, I would be patient and let them go at their own pace—this time allotting plenty of time to be flexible. Granted, I still have my moments and am far from a perfect mom, but learning to let go of my sense of urgency has made everyone's morning a little bit better.

—*Julia*

CHAPTER TWO
Tracks

FINDING *your* WAY HOME

It was my mom's idea for me to take the train from Springfield to Joliet. Winter was cold that year, like most winters in Illinois. And I wasn't sure how I was going to get home for Christmas.

Without a car at college, I often had to find creative ways to travel during the holidays. Sometimes, my parents would drive the three and a half hours downstate via I-39 to pick me up; other times, I'd have to find my own way, usually catching a ride with a friend. But this year, all my friends were busy, and none were headed in the vicinity of my hometown. This didn't bother me, though, as holidays were often stressful. Deciding I'd stay put, I called my mom to tell her the news. She wasn't interested. Instead, she proposed an alternative solution: *take the train.*

I loved the idea. Aside from some anxiety about spending all winter break at home, cooped up, it sounded exciting. In those days, I was especially restless; hardly able to stand still, always looking to the next thing. And a train ride sounded like the adventure I'd been craving. So I told her I'd do it.

A senior with only a semester of school left, I was eager to get on with the rest of life but at the same time, nervous about the future. This was the time to decide what I was going to do after graduation, but I felt stuck. Three weeks at home sounded like a waste of perfectly good time to be *doing*. I could've spent the break traveling or hanging out with friends from school, but instead I'd be shoveling snow and having awkward run-ins with old friends. I was headed home. And if I was going to be dragged back there, at least I'd be taking the train.

The last train I'd been on was in Europe, the previous year. Before leaving the States for my semester in Spain, I received a gift from my grandma, who was a travel agent. She bought my friend and me what became our most prized possessions that semester: Eurail passes. With them, we could board nearly any train in the continent and go wherever our wanderlust took us. So we did just that, every chance we had.

During our travels in Europe, every day was a new and exciting experience. We relished the sights, sounds, and smells: ancient cathedrals and castles; exotic foods, languages, and customs; and more than a few wonders of the world. These were the experiences of a lifetime, and they filled more than a few photo albums now sitting on my mother's bookshelves.

Despite all the unbelievable sights—and bragging rights I acquired as a result of seeing them—the images most indelibly ingrained in my mind from that semester were the subtle ones. The candy kiosks in the Seville station. The aloof Frenchman issuing train tickets from a small kiosk in Nice. The Tolkien-like, trench-coated character we shared a car with in Genoa. Despite some of the grandiose moments we had, what I recall most clearly from our travels was the waiting. Delays and postponements. Random run-ins with strangers we'd never see again. Day trips through cities while waiting for our next departure. And of course, the time on the trains. Most prominent among my memories of Europe weren't the destinations themselves but the times and places in between.

Having been through all that, you'd think I would have been better at waiting in all these in-between times by now. But I wasn't. As I booked my tickets for the trip home that winter—almost exactly a year after my European adventure—I couldn't wait to board another train, hoping to relive some of those recent but slowly fading memories.

In Europe, taking the train is usually faster and more efficient than traveling by car or bus. However, I loved riding them for their elegance, not their speed. The fact that you got where you were going more quickly was just an added bonus. Riding the train made me feel classy and very James Bond–like. Whenever boarding one,

I'd look to find one of those blocks of four seats facing each other with a table in the middle—perfect for top-secret conversations about international espionage.

I hadn't been on a train since studying abroad, but I assumed the American version of the experience would be similar. After being car-less for nearly four years, I was becoming fond of slower, more deliberate forms of travel. And given my jaunt home for the holidays—where I wouldn't have the same freedoms and carefree schedule as in college—I could use a few extra hours to prepare for the following weeks.

But there was one crucial difference between American trains and European ones—and it had nothing to do with the trains themselves. Trains in Europe had always taken me someplace new and unfamiliar. They allowed me to see more of the world, giving me opportunities to grow. But now I was using one to go home, the one place I'd been avoiding all these years. Having been in the same country for over a year and thus, fairly stable for over a year, my skin was starting to crawl. Many of my friends had graduated and moved on to their careers, and I felt caught in between two major moments in life. No matter how much it pained me, all I could do was wait for the next exciting season to begin. So the thought of choosing to stay in one place for any duration of time was repulsive.

I paid a friend ten bucks for gas money to drive me from Jacksonville to Springfield—a thirty-minute trip when the weather was nice. The news said a snowstorm had recently hit Northern Illinois, but downstate things were still good. Another reason I didn't want to go home: the weather. Although the distance wasn't great, the trip home felt like a cross-cultural experience. People talked differently up there, acted differently. And I was starting to identify more with where I lived, not where I was from.

Arriving at the Amtrak station a few hours early, I claimed my ticket from will-call and pulled out a book while I waited. When the train pulled into the station, I sprang from my seat and raced to be first in line. As soon as I boarded, I glanced around the car, then frowned. Where were all the seats facing each other? Where was the bar? Where were the men wearing suits, reading newspapers? Where was James Bond? The bench seats were lined up in rows like on a bus, and the walls were lined with a rug-like material that was dated and torn.

I sighed, disappointed.

The train was far from full. Despite the many empty seats, I decided to slide into a bench next to an elderly man. His clothes were neat and tidy; he wore a white, collared shirt with a bow tie, gray vest, and a dark gray cabbie hat. And he was clutching a bouquet of flowers. Staring at the floor, the man didn't notice my entrance until I squeezed past him to take the window seat. Every chance I had while traveling, I sat near windows, never wanting to miss a thing.

"Hello," I said.

"Hello," he said, his head jerking up.

The man cracked a smile, then returned to staring at the floor. For the first thirty minutes, those were the only words we exchanged. I had my window seat, which was enough for me, and he seemed to be in his own world. Making myself comfortable, I pulled out my journal and began taking notes as the world I knew vanished and a new one came into view.

Fields full of snow and sparsely populated towns lined the rails. A few birds had chosen not to migrate and sat perched atop phone lines running along the tracks. Rolling my eyes at the less-than-spectacular view, I decided to read for a bit. After skimming a few pages with my head propped against the cold glass, I fell asleep. Drifting off to the sounds of train wheels on iron track, I thought of past Illinois winters of my childhood . . . and how I hated them.

I was eleven, maybe twelve, and my family had just moved from the suburbs of Chicago to a small farm town with a population of eleven hundred. That day, my parents had gotten into a fight, and to get back at my dad, my mom hid his Mickey Mantle baseball card. When I discovered this, I was outraged, because the card wasn't just my dad's. It was mine. *Ours.* He held on to it for me—to keep it safe—but it belonged to both of us.

Marching up to my mother, who was cooking in the kitchen, I demanded, "Give me back my card."

"Stay out of this, Jeffery," she scolded, using my full first name (never a good sign).

"No. That's my card. I want it back."

She rolled her eyes, continuing to stir something in the pot on the stove.

"Mom!" I said. "I want my card back. *Give* it to me!"

"Jeff, this is between your father and me. Stay out of it."

Then she left the stove and began to walk out of the kitchen. I stood in her way, trying to block her, but she brushed past my preteen body, uninterested in negotiations. This made me even angrier.

Seething, I did the only thing I could to regain control of the situation: I decided to steal my mom's favorite pair of earrings. She didn't have much jewelry and often lost necklaces and other pieces, but for some reason she had hung on to these earrings. They weren't expensive or fancy, but they were her favorite nonetheless.

Disappearing into her bedroom while she folded clothes in the living room, I rummaged through her jewelry box while watching the door, paranoid of being caught. Eyes on the entryway, I fished out a few unwanted sets until . . . *there*. I'd found them. With the earrings in hand, I quietly closed the jewelry drawer and then the bedroom door behind me, then stepped out the back door into the cold, without a coat.

"Oh, Moooom!" I called in my best Macaulay Culkin voice, daring her to come see me do something horrible.

At first she didn't hear, so I raised my voice and shouted again.

This time, she came to the back door and saw me standing in the snow. "What do you *want*?" She sounded annoyed.

Good, I thought. *Let her be mad.*

"Give me back my card," I said.

"Stay out of this, Jeff. It's between me and Dad." She went to close the door.

"No! That's *my* card; give it back. Or I'll throw these."

I pulled my arm back like a catapult threatening to launch. Standing in the snow with unlaced snow boots, I felt the cold creep up my legs while sweat dripped down my forehead.

"What?" she asked, squinting to see what was in my hand. And then—she saw. Her eyes widened and seemed to darken a hue. "If you even dare . . ."

I accepted the challenge and released the catapult.

———————

"It's beautiful, isn't it?" The man's voice startled me from sleep.

I twisted my neck to look at him, my eyes refocusing. Looking out the window of the train, I was disappointed to see the same boring countryside as before. How long had I been out? Maybe half an hour?

I cleared my throat. "What is?"

"That," he answered, nodding toward the scene outside the window.

The empty cornfields, the handfuls of trees and houses, the occasional telephone pole — the world passing us by, all covered in white. I didn't get it.

"I guess."

It was, after all, nothing compared to the seaside view from Monaco at night. It paled in contrast to the city life of Rome that greeted me early one September morning. And it was nothing like the train ride from Nice to Barcelona. Just another unremarkable ride through the countryside of Illinois. What was so great about that?

I'd always hated my state, but in winter I loathed it. Everything was dead and frozen and miserable. When I was a teenager, winter meant early mornings of shoveling snow, often missing the bottom frozen layer, and then having to throw salt to melt the ice. It meant chapped lips and cold sores, cracked-dry knuckles and starting the car twenty minutes before needing to go anywhere. It meant slipping on sidewalks and sliding through four-way stops. I hated winter.

This antipathy probably came from my dad, a completely warm-blooded creature. One winter, he fell down a flight of stairs while shoveling the entryway to our townhouse. He had trouble getting around for months after that. When I became old enough, shoveling the walkway became my responsibility, and after that I dreaded every snowfall.

Winter also meant Christmas. Not the Disney Channel kind, though. The Griswold kind with an ironic twist, leaving someone crying at the end of the day. It meant getting presents we didn't want from relatives we didn't know and driving through blizzards for awkward exchanges over potluck dinners.

Every winter came with defrosters and dehumidifiers, snow-drifts and shorter days; it meant slowing down in a small town that already went too slow for my taste.

I hated winter.

"I work with flowers," the man said with a self-assured smile. I furrowed my brow, and he clarified: "I'm a florist!"

"Really?"

He nodded, lifting the bouquet in his hands for me to see. Roses. Red ones. Dark and deep, the kind of hues only possible on a movie set. I wondered how one acquired such beautiful flowers in winter.

"They're for my wife," he said, looking down for a moment. Then he returned his gaze. "Are you married?"

I shook my head, not sure if I'd ever get married.

"Well, it's great. You'll see," he said with a wink and a grin.

"Do you live in Joliet?" I asked, trying to change the subject.

The man shook his head. "No. I'm visiting my—" He stopped, his face growing flushed, and then resumed, "*our*—daughter."

I nodded, ignoring his embarrassment or whatever it was.

Looking down, he returned the question in a quieter voice, "And you?"

"I live close. My parents are picking me up. I'm visiting for Christmas."

He nodded, smiling. *What was he smiling about?*

"I'm a college student," I explained, "and we're on break, so I kind of *have* to go."

"That's great," he said, sighing. Then he paused, as if in thought, before saying, "There's nothing like going home."

He turned away for a moment, looking out the window across the aisle. For a second, I thought I saw a tear or two pool in his eyes, but then he turned back to resume the conversation.

As the rural landscape crept by, we continued chatting. The train had to be going half the pace as the ones in Europe, but I didn't mind. In fact, I was looking for any reason to delay going home, and I was actually starting to enjoy the conversation with the florist. He asked what I was studying in school and what my family was like, and I got to hear about his daughter and her family, how excited he was to become a grandfather. But nothing about his wife. We filled the silence as best we could, and I enjoyed the company, but I can't recall more than those details. What hung with me—and even haunted me—were those five words: *There's nothing like going home.*

As we neared Chicago, the stops became more frequent, and the city lights brightened. The landscape transitioned from rural to metropolitan, and the quiet solitude of cornfields was replaced with the hustle and bustle of city life and suburban busyness. I knew what this meant. We were almost to Joliet.

By now, I'd grown accustomed to the scratchy fabric in the seats, and had even let myself sink into them, wanting the train ride to continue. It wasn't Europe, but it was still sort of novel. As we neared the end of our train ride together, I grew anxious, and all my stressors returned. *What would I do about the job I'd just applied for? Would I hear back about teaching English in China next year? And what about Christmas? Would it be another debacle or could it actually be enjoyable this year?*

Realizing I'd spent most of the train ride dominating the conversation, I started asking the florist more questions—both to distract me from the anxiety of what was to come and because I was genuinely interested.

"Are you excited to see your wife?"

"Well," he squirmed. "Yes . . . I suppose."

I frowned. "Well, I'm sure she's excited to see you—and those flowers!"

He looked down at the roses and nodded in surprise as if he'd forgotten he was holding them. Then he looked away for a moment before glancing back at me. He forced a smile.

"Yes, I'm sure she is." Again, he looked away, and I swear I saw tears.

"Do you guys visit your daughter every year for Christmas?"

"Yes . . . well, I do. I visit both my daughter and my wife."

"What do you mean? She doesn't live with you?" I was starting to get nosy.

"No. I mean, yes. Well, she, ah . . . well, she's . . . *gone*."

"Oh." And then I didn't know what else to say.

We arrived in Joliet several minutes ahead of schedule. I thanked the florist for sharing with me and wished him a Merry Christmas. Then I grabbed my suitcase and made my way toward the exit.

I had not been looking forward to this visit. Going home was hard now, because home was no longer where I grew up. It was somewhere *out there*—in Spain or Italy, maybe even Texas. But not here, not in boring, bitter-cold Illinois. Home was out on the open road, waiting to be discovered—not with family and familiar places. It was on train rides and Portuguese beaches, stuffed into the fibers of all things exotic and different.

As I exited the train car, the florist called to me with what sounded like feigned cheeriness, "Enjoy your family!"

I smiled and turned to leave, thinking about those words again: *There's nothing like going home.* Searching for my mom in the crowd of people reuniting at the train station, I remembered where I was the previous year.

While spending Thanksgiving in Spain, eating poor substitutes for pumpkin pie, I called home — not to tell my family I missed them, but to inform them I'd be traveling over New Year's Eve to attend a conference. I wouldn't be home for long during the break, I told my mom. After spending the past four months in Spain and the previous three in Texas, I was going to be gone again soon. Mom sounded upset, and I didn't know why. *What was her problem, anyway? Didn't she understand I didn't belong there anymore, that the world was too big for me to stay in one place for too long? Especially that place—home.*

"Home is where I lay my head," I told my boss at camp the previous summer.

Even then, it sounded ridiculous. When I left home years ago, I wanted more than cornfields and community college. I wanted an adventure that was bigger than me. Home was a fleeting feeling, a passing moment; it wasn't something constant to return to after years of travel or a semester at school. Home was wherever I decided to be.

Thinking back to the day I released my mom's earrings into the snow, I knew I was wrong.

She didn't react as expected. She just walked away. Standing in the snow, a smug look on my face, I had won. A moment later, my mom reappeared at the back door, holding what looked like a baseball card in her hands. Without a word, she threw the plastic-coated portrait of Mickey Mantle in my direction and slammed the door, locking it behind her.

Running through the snow and almost losing my boots, I retrieved the card. As I picked it up, I sighed in relief, seeing it was undamaged by the snow. Finally, I had gotten what I wanted. My plan had worked—so why did I feel so rotten?

As the weight of what I'd done hit me, I ran back into the yard, trudging through six inches of snow, to find the earrings. After searching for nearly an hour, I never found them. Resigned, I returned to the back porch, wondering how to get back in. Surprised to see the door unlocked, I entered and shed my boots, quietly brushing the ice off my pant legs. Then I crept downstairs to my bedroom, hoping I could go to bed without having to face anyone, especially my mom. My plan was to slip out in the morning to search again for earrings.

A few hours later, my mom called me for dinner.

Great, I thought. *This is going to be bad.*

To my shock, she didn't say anything about the card or the earrings. Unsmiling, she served me my dinner—probably something like meatloaf—and didn't say a word. I could tell she was mad. So why wasn't she saying anything?

We shared a warm meal together—the whole family—and few words were exchanged. I don't recall my mom bringing up the matter to my dad or shaming me with what I'd done. We just ate, each person quietly keeping to himself. I even had seconds.

Later, I would apologize to Mom. I would do this many times, even pleading for forgiveness. And of course, she forgave me, saying it was okay. But I knew it wasn't. How could it be? Those were her favorite earrings. And although I tried to make up for my crime with other gifts and forms of retribution, I couldn't. The damage was done. Forever.

For days after, I would return to the backyard to scan the area for the earrings, hoping the old pair would turn up. But they never did. Even after the snow melted and winter passed, I never found them.

Those earrings taught me an obvious lesson about consequences and why we sometimes can't undo the hurt we cause others. Years later, though, while riding on a train, I learned another lesson about what it means to go home.

Home is the place where we sometimes hurt the ones we love, but the back door is always open — and there is always a seat at the table. We have a choice where we put our hearts and lay our heads, but home is where it's always been. Home is *home* — not necessarily a location, but more than a feeling. It's the place where we are loved, even when that love is complicated and messy but still sets a place at the table for you.

Returning home that winter break, while thinking of things like college and careers and the coming future, I realized there was no place I'd rather be waiting.

As I stepped off the platform, letting my feet hit the concrete sidewalk, I saw the sun was setting and could hear Christmas music playing somewhere in the distance. It was starting to get cold, but I had never felt warmer. Looking across the crowds of reuniting families, I saw my mom standing in the distance, waiting for me.

She was smiling.

That winter, my restlessness could not be tempered or controlled; it nearly consumed me. I wanted to move on to the next thing or return to the previous adventure. But I couldn't. I was stuck on a ride that went more slowly than it should have. As with the train, I was beginning to appreciate the pace, because it was moving at just the right speed. I was learning to take my time, to live in the tension between where I was and wanted to be.

What better place to do that than with the familiar? With family?

Home. It's where we take things for granted and sometimes do things we're not proud of. Where we cry and scream and always have a hot meal waiting for us. It's the one place that never really goes away; it's always there, wherever *there* may be.

And it's the perfect place to return to.

Pulling my luggage behind me, I greeted my mom with a hug and thought to myself:

There's nothing like going home.

IN-BETWEEN GLIMPSES

Eighteen years ago my daughter revealed that her stepdad was sexually abusing her. In all the fallout afterward, I waited, prayed, and worked toward healing. Three years passed before the sun began to shine again on our lives, and many more years passed before complete healing happened for all family members. In the waiting, I grew closer to God and stronger in my faith. I learned to ask God, "What do You have for me to learn from this situation?" rather than demanding, "Why did You let this happen?"

—Debra

CHAPTER THREE
The Road

LOVING *the* JOURNEY

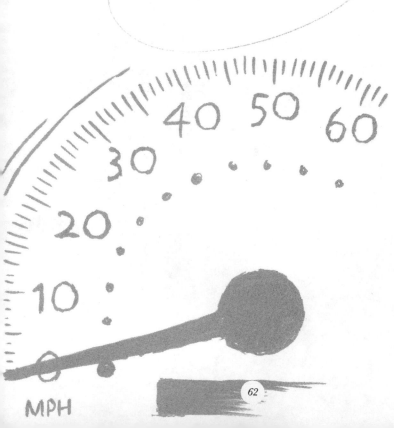

40 50 60

30

20

10

0

MPH

After graduating college, I spent the greater part of a year traveling around North America, playing with a band. For nine months, we lived on the road. Every day, we moved from place to place, living out of a fifteen-passenger van in between our short stops. Expecting a year full of adventure and travel, I leaped into the unknown, ready for anything. Little did I know, that year of travel was going to give me a first-class education in waiting.

That year, I saw Niagara Falls and the Statue of Liberty, hiked the Rockies and strolled through an old monastery in California, slept in mansions and on hardwood floors. I saw it all. But before that, I saw a show with my friend Paul.

A few months before graduation, around the same time I met my wife, a time when I was trying to figure out my future, I received an offer to teach English in China. Everything was set—I had a job, a place to live, and my living expenses covered for the next two years—but I was having second thoughts. It was, as they say, the opportunity of a lifetime, but something felt wrong.

I was having doubts the day that Paul called, asking if I wanted to see a live show with him that night. Paul and I had played in a couple of groups on campus—he on drums and me on guitar—and often went to concerts together. Whether it was some new indie band he was into or an old staple we both loved, we always had a great time. This night, I was especially hoping to get lost in the music.

Paul picked me up at my house around six that night. As we drove down College Avenue, he asked about my postgrad opportunities. Paul was a year older than me and had been a mentor of sorts, so I valued his opinion. He rarely gave advice, though, usually only listening and asking the occasional question. Despite the fact that Paul was usually the smartest guy in the room, you'd never know it; he was humble. I wanted him to tell me what to do, but I knew better than to expect that. When I told him about my doubts, he just nodded, narrowing his eyes as if deep in thought.

For as long as I had known him, Paul had mutton chops—big, thick sideburns threatening to overtake his face—which he had recently tamed and transformed into a more respectable form of facial hair: a goatee. Having finished his first year of seminary, Paul had adopted a new look, which I figured was a sign of a more serious outlook on life.

When I asked my friend how seminary was going, he told me he was having his own doubts about life and the direction in which he was headed. But that was all I could get out of him, because by then we had arrived at MacMurray College to see the show.

Toward the end of the concert, just before the last song, one of the singers invited any musicians in the crowd to come see the band afterwards. As the last song concluded, I looked to Paul, waiting to see if he went forward, before I made my move. Without hesitation, he did, and I reluctantly followed. When I introduced myself to the band, the guitarist took me back to another room and asked me to play a few things. Then he thanked me, and I left, returning to the first room where Paul was finishing up his audition, concluding with a flawless drum solo. I sighed. Sometimes, I hated that guy.

During the drive home, Paul and I discussed how cool it'd be to tour together. Throughout the four years we'd known each other, this had always been a dream of ours: to go out on the road as bandmates. After that night, though, I forgot about the experience, thinking it was a long shot, and returned to worrying about what to do with China.

A few weeks later, I received a phone call from a woman named Melody who worked for the organization that sponsored the group we had seen. She had seen my audition and liked it. She wanted to know if I'd be interested in joining a team next year. I wondered if she had the wrong guy. She assured me they'd be glad to have me and told me to take some time to think about it.

I didn't know what to do. The idea of touring with a real band excited me; I had waited for this chance ever since I picked up a guitar at sixteen. But teaching in China was part of the plan, and it was a good plan that promised its own set of adventures. One opportunity tugged at my heart while the other weighed on my conscience. Did I follow my heart or trust my instincts?

"God can use you anywhere," my friend the schoolteacher told me. I didn't believe it. I believed God had a plan that could be seriously messed up if I didn't pay attention. But maybe it was true. Did God call me to Spain? Did He tell me to date that girl who broke my heart not once or even twice, but three times? (The fourth time, I broke hers.) No, but somehow He helped me make the most of those situations.

Maybe, I thought, *God is less concerned with exactly what I'm doing and more concerned with who I'm becoming.*

When Paul told me Melody had called him too, I wasn't surprised. Without hesitation, he decided to go for it. Despite my agonizing over China, I felt inspired by his whimsy, and just like that, I followed my friend's lead—as did two of our other friends. All four of us would spend the next eleven months on three domestic tours and one international stint, playing music all over the world. It would be an experience we'd never forget, but not for the reasons we expected.

In August, my dad drove me to Minnesota, where I would begin my year of travel. There, I met my three friends from college, plus eleven strangers. The group immediately began to gel, and Paul and I assumed control. In between bouts of rehearsal, we initiated movie nights and pickup games of ultimate Frisbee.

Little did I know, I was setting the stage for what the rest of the year would hold.

One day a few weeks before our first tour, our road manager, Chris, invited Paul and me out to lunch. Over hamburgers and milkshakes at Culver's, he told us we would make good leaders, that we should each lead one of the two teams.

Paul accepted the position. And I did the same, though with reservation. Paul had always been more comfortable with leadership, and I usually assumed the "number two" role. He was the friendly, outgoing guy who pulled people together to create memorable experiences; I was the shy one who warmed up after hanging out a few times. That's the way it had always been.

But this time was different. This time, I'd be on one side of the country, and Paul would be on the other. Who would I look up to? Who would help me make major decisions? I guess that person was me. Now, I'd have to figure it out on my own.

As the time to leave for tour drew near, I secretly wished and waited for someone to say I wouldn't have to go. Maybe another leader would show up to replace me and I could join my friend Paul, where I belonged. But no one ever came.

So I packed my bag, took a deep breath, and hit the road. Our team headed east, and Paul's went west.

The first tour was full of experiences, but I barely slowed down to notice them. First, we drove as far north as Toronto, where we played a series of shows for a group of Chinese churches. After that, we spent a day at Niagara Falls. Then we headed south, passing through New York and stopping in Washington, D.C., where we performed one morning at an inner-city school that was blocks away from the Capitol building. It took us three hours to get out of the city because of a bomb scare. In Virginia, we were treated to a night at a four-star hotel where Martha Washington supposedly

THE ROAD: LOVING THE JOURNEY

stayed. We'd play shows for audiences as large as twelve hundred people, but I often felt alone. What should have been an incredible first tour was one I struggled to appreciate. The more we toured, the more restless I became, wanting to move on to the next place.

Every morning, we'd wake up in a new host home. Just before sunrise, we'd pack our suitcases, throw them into the back of our Ford Econoline, and head out to the next destination. Some families would wake with us and hand out Styrofoam cups full of coffee along with a breakfast burrito or English muffin. As the main driver, I'd shuttle our conversion van around from house to house, picking up each member of the band. Sometimes, honking out front wasn't enough; sometimes, I had to go into the house and wake my teammates, even pull them out of bed. I didn't sign up to be a parent, but that's what the job required, sometimes. Then we'd spend the next six to twelve hours on the road.

That year, I realized how large my country is and how many flat roads and cornfields it contains. In order to pass the time, we always had music playing. Our sound engineer had an eclectic taste, so we often stole his iPod to get acquainted with new bands. We'd arrive at our gig around dinnertime, and I'd fill the empty space in the day with phone calls back to our home office or to contacts for upcoming gigs. Each night, we'd play a show, meet our new family for the evening, have a late dinner, and fall into bed, exhausted. The next morning, the cycle would start over.

Halfway through the tour, our drummer started dating one of the vocalists. The relationship caused jealousy and bitterness within the team, and as the leader I didn't know how to handle it. Trying to control it, I was domineering to a fault, which only backfired, making the situation worse. Seeing that what I was doing wasn't working, I distanced myself emotionally from the situation, growing more ambivalent as time went on. I gave up. Was this the adventure I'd been waiting for? Surely not. It seemed an awful lot like the life I was trying to escape. I was dealing with the same issues I imagined my peers who had become bankers and schoolteachers were facing.

In addition to the dating drama and awkward team dynamics, we had other problems: shows that flopped and occasional vehicular mishaps. Apparently, guitars don't stay in tune in the winter and traffic pylons don't jump out of your way when you're barreling down I-55 in a fifteen-passenger conversion van. I was sure all this—the relational conflicts, the missed key changes, even the mutilated pylons in the south suburbs of Chicago—was my fault. And this sense of guilt made me feel even more alone.

The loneliness led me to spend a day off in New York City. We had less than twenty-four hours before our next gig, so most of the team spent the day at home, watching movies and catching up on email, but I already felt disconnected from the group. So why not actually leave? A few of us had never been to the Big Apple before, so we decided to take advantage of the downtime, taking a train into downtown. Despite the fact that some of them were fifty or a hundred years old, every building and street had a sheen of novelty. The movies didn't lie; this was a magical city. Overwhelmed with new sights and smells, I barely noticed the incessant rainfall that endured the whole day. For the first time in a long time, I didn't feel alone.

Staring up at the Empire State Building and down into the abyss of Ground Zero, I was overwhelmed with a strange comfort: I realized my own insignificance. The words of a Jimmy Eat World song came to mind. *I am but one small instrument.*[4] My problems seemed tiny in light of the millions passing by, with little concern or notice for my issues. I had no loss worth lamenting, no cross to bear that compared to the thousands who'd lost their lives on 9/11. For some reason, these macabre thoughts gave me hope to continue, to keep going when I wanted to quit.

As I consumed a Gray's Papaya hot dog, the rain pelted my city map into oblivion, and I felt oddly connected with the universe. I was anonymous, just another passerby; yet, I knew there was another story happening, one bigger than my own problems. Something deep and primal in my soul reminded me of this. As my fingers gripped the chain-link fence that surrounded the site of the Twin Towers, I gazed in complete awe at the place where thousands of souls breathed their last. In this heaviness, I found a certain lightness that set me free.

Hope came in the form of St. Paul's Chapel, a centuries-old church that had miraculously survived the terrorist attacks on September 11, 2001 — despite the fact that it was in the heart of Ground Zero. I'd heard about this little place of worship, seen it on television and read about it on the Internet, but seeing it in person was a different experience altogether.

It's a small, old building   a miniature plaything in contrast to the hulking skyscrapers that surround it — and a bit odd-looking, made for a different era before airplanes and highways. Yet, it remains, refusing to conform to the pressures of modern architecture. Words don't do it justice, but that little chapel tells a story of redemption that remains with me years after the fact. It was what I needed to persevere, to find hope in an unlikely place.

Our year was full of little moments like that. In fact, more than the big concerts and long hours of travel, the hushed gaps between scheduled events remain strongest in my memory. These were the moments reminding me that God cared more about who I was becoming than what I was doing at the time.

We had big moments and great achievements, too. There was the time we raced our van around the Bristol Motor Speedway.

ough the Appalachians. There were the shows when
ʌr thousands of people and got to see lives changed.
ɔut in light of St. Paul's, these were relatively insignificant snippets in a larger story. What we did was not as important as who we were becoming. And I had a feeling that the folks back at the office—our booking agent, our road manager, our finance person—were concerned about this, too. This wasn't a story of arriving, but of waiting. We waited to arrive at our next location, waited to play our next show, waited to eat our next meal. Even I was waiting to be the kind of person who deserved to lead such a team. And those small, slow moments that caused me to pause and reflect became the bedrock of my growth that year.

By November, my team and I had made it through our first tour. It was an adjustment for us all and harder than expected. We had embarked on this tour with idealistic expectations for what it would look like to live on the road, form our own community, and play for live crowds. We returned from the trip with those ideals ravaged by reality. What was left standing was a rather normal-looking vocation, despite the seemingly abnormal context, full of its share of faults and frustrations. It looked a lot like the lives we'd hoped to leave behind. We had each given up some other opportunity in exchange for the chance to travel and see the world, and despite all our moving around, we seemed to be standing still.

After Christmas, we headed west to California, and Paul's team went east, Florida-bound. Sometime after navigating through the Rockies and traversing the beaches of San Diego, I learned another lesson in becoming. For me, I thought the year was about playing music, about what we had to offer. But soon I would find out the opposite was true: that when we pour out our gifts and talents, we receive abundantly more than we ever provide.

That spring, my team spent a week in Seattle, driving hours each day to the far-stretching parts of Washington state to play live shows for convicted felons. We played mostly in prisons, visiting penitentiary after penitentiary to the point that we could have done the security checks in our sleep. During the long van rides back to the city, after hours of setting up, playing, tearing down, and moving on, we'd listen to the folk ballads of Damien Rice and look out at the night sky, contemplatively, thinking we had done some good deed.

One time, we were introduced to a group of men who had no chance of parole. "Lifers," I think they were called, and these men belonged to a special subgroup of prisoners that the chaplain called the "God Pod." They would never know life outside of bars and concrete walls, a fact they seemed to disregard as this was the most spiritually passionate group of men I'd ever met.

They asked us to lead a church worship service for the group, but it would only be fair to say we *attempted* to lead such a service. Plugging in our instruments, we did a sound check and prepared to share our musical gifts with these men. But before we played a single note, the Lifers entered the room and filled the empty space with their voices, singing, "Amazing grace, how sweet the sound ..."

It was this way with every song: we'd strum the first chord in a song, the men would start nodding along, and soon their voices would drown out ours. As I strummed my electric guitar through an amplifier that bounced the sound off the concrete walls, I realized this group could teach me something. In a former life, these men were rapists and murderers—people who had committed the vilest acts of humanity—and here they were, singing songs about forgiveness and redemption. First, I thought the situation ironic; but then I concluded if anyone ever deserved to sing of such topics with such gusto, they did.

The experience was an apparition, haunting me like a shadow long after we left Seattle. On long nights driving through the Cascade Mountains, I'd stare into the black tundra, hearing those passionate *a cappella* pleas for grace once again. And when everyone was asleep and I was sure only God could hear, I would join them.

The end of the tour was anticlimactic. We had a handful of stops in Idaho and North Dakota, but these were "filler" experiences for me. As far as I was concerned, the tour was done and we were on our way home. I was already beginning to check out, planning what I'd be doing the following year. It wasn't until one night in Montana that I woke back up.

Although I can barely remember their faces, I'll never forget the hospitality one couple showed us during an overnight stay in Billings, a small mountain town in the Northern Rockies. We rolled into town late that night due to a bad snowstorm. Behind schedule, we couldn't even bother stopping for supper.

Rolling into Billings around eight-thirty, I figured there'd be at least one restaurant still open. But I was wrong. Apparently, the whole town, even the grocery store, shuts down after dark. I asked our host, John, where we could find something to eat, and he laughed. Then he took me to a bar, the only place that was still open. When we asked what they had to eat, the bartender explained the grill was closed and all they had were tiny frozen pizzas.

John shook his head as if that simply would not do.

"Come with me," he said with a sigh.

He brought me to the church that he pastored and showed me the pantry full of donated food. With a proper amount of piety, I protested. *Wasn't this food for the needy?* He started throwing boxes of macaroni and cheese into a box. When he heard me argue, he stopped and stared at me, his brow furrowed. He didn't look mad, just disappointed. Saying nothing, I nodded in resignation to the fact that we were, indeed, those needy people for whom the pantry was intended. He continued dumping food into a cardboard box.

When he was finished, the pastor presented our haul: a few loaves of Wonder bread, several packages of American cheese, a half dozen boxes of macaroni, and several cans of mixed vegetables and fruit cocktail. We brought the box back to the house, and John's wife proceeded to unpack each item, setting it on the kitchen counter. With ravenous eyes, we watched her prepare a feast: dozens of grilled cheese sandwiches, each stained with the proper amount of real butter; mountains of macaroni and creamy orange cheese sauce; and plenty of vegetables and syrup-soaked fruit for dessert. Maybe it was due to the fact that we hadn't eaten anything in eight hours, but I don't recall food ever tasting so good.

The next morning, Pastor John brought us all back to the church, where we ate a breakfast of pancakes and sausage prepared by members of the congregation. A few parishioners wheeled out an old upright piano and asked us to sing a few hymns. Willingly, we obliged. This time, we all sang and played beautifully — even on an out-of-tune piano, everything seemed to sound right. No bad notes; no negative emotions. Next to the prison service in Seattle, I'd never been part of a more sincere service.

These were simple people who wore flannel shirts and closed their shops before six o'clock on weeknights. They didn't follow the latest trends in music or read cutting-edge literature on the relevance of rock bands in churches. But they knew how to love people. As we concluded our set with the hymn "How Great Thou Art," I looked around at my teammates — the people I'd been embittered toward and angry with for much of the year — and realized that the beauty of community rests in its fragility. These people weren't perfect, and neither was I. But what else did we have, other than each other?

Rolling into Willmar, where our journey began nearly nine months before, we stopped at Jake's Pizza for several larges. As we sat around the table exchanging stories, I didn't realize it, but I would never have a moment like this again. Not with these people. We'd never get to laugh like this or tease each other; after that day, it would be different. We had another tour ahead of us, and then we would go our separate ways for the summer, some of us never seeing each other again.

If I had known this was the last time, I probably would have said something memorable. But instead I asked my friend Wes to pass me another slice.

That summer, Paul and I got together one last time. Having spent so much time apart, we had a lot to talk about. As we swapped stories, we realized how similar they were. He told me the ways he had failed and the things he saw in me that he'd grown to admire. I still looked up to him, but now, maybe for the first time, we were peers. And that felt empowering. I was no longer the backup guy, the number two. I'd become my own man, a leader.

That year on the road changed me. No longer afraid to lead, I saw no need to hide behind someone else's shadow. I had grown up. And it wouldn't have happened if it weren't for the waiting. All those experiences that frustrated me to no end were the ones that taught me the most. They showed me the value of sticking with commitments and how to love the people around me, no matter who they were. And most of all, they taught me how to do hard things — which is what growing up is all about.

When we go on a journey, we're often not sure how it will end, and this is the point. We travel to remember we are not done. Although there are destination points, what matters is that we stay on the road. What I remember from that year even now is not any one of the hundreds of destinations. The moments that remain fixed in my mind are the minor ones, the memories that fell in between the major stops: the post-9/11 walk through New York, the macaroni dinner in Montana, the sounds of condemned men singing praise songs in prison walls. Those were the times that taught me the most that year. And they're the ones that still do today.

IN-BETWEEN GLIMPSES

After being laid off more than two years ago, I was waiting for clarity and answers. Those answers took on so many different forms during this "valley." They came in the form of finding satisfaction from things like coaching my five-year-old son's soccer team instead of hearing, "You're hired!" They came in the form of laying out a foundation to start my own speaking business. I'm still waiting, by the way . . . but the transformation has already begun.

—Romeo

part two

WORTH *the* WAIT

Christmas Eve. The perfect picture of anticipation: sleepless excitement for something we've been waiting all year for. Every year on December 24, my parents let us open a present. This was a teaser, a taste of things to come, and we kids relished it. Of course, it wasn't much of a surprise—my mom almost always got us new pajamas, even when we didn't need them. But still, it was a ritual of hope, one in which we celebrated the gift of giving, the joy of gratitude.

Christmas morning. An unfortunate picture of disappointment. I am obviously only one person with his own set of experiences, but as I talk to others, I find similar feelings of frustration. As they get older, many people seem to develop a general distrust toward any day that promises to fill the emptiness they've felt all year long. This explains the rise in suicides during this season and why, for some, Christmas is a reminder of the inevitable letdown of life. The unfortunate answer to the question, "Did you get everything you wanted?" is, of course, no. And we feel terrible about this. Why can't we be happy? Why can't we be satisfied? Will we ever be content with what we have—with the gifts in our stockings, the toys under the tree? Why is there this constant thirst for *more*?

Maybe the answer lies in the night before the big day.

When I was in Spain, Loli told me Christmas Day is important in her culture but not celebrated the same way as in the US. The more she said, the more I wondered if there was some hidden wisdom in how the Spaniards celebrate Christmas. She said her family gets together on December 24, *La Noche Buena* ("The Good Night"), and has a church service, sometimes followed by a gift exchange. The day, though, isn't about gift giving; it's about celebration and commemoration, feasting and family. It's a day that's not about "me" but rather "us"—about being together, not getting things.

This was a revelation to me, that an entire culture could avoid the pressure placed on a day typically about consumption and refocus it on slowing down. Instead of spiraling into credit card debt and frantically rushing around to pick up last-minute gifts, they simply enjoy the time they have together. Wow. Of course, that's not to say the Spanish don't give gifts; they do. On January 6, they—and many others around the world—celebrate Epiphany, a holiday I heard nothing about while growing up in the Midwest. This is the Day of the Magi, when the wise men traditionally brought gifts of frankincense, gold, and myrrh to baby Jesus. For many cultures around the world, this is when the gifts come.

So what are they doing for those two weeks in between Christmas and Epiphany? Waiting, of course.

Although we had several Bibles in our home while I was growing up, I didn't often open one—except around Christmas. Every December, I'd peel back the leather cover of my dad's Bible and read the story of Jesus' birth. I'm not sure what drew me to it; I think I just knew there was something important in that detail that I was missing on TV and in the stories playing out around me. And although I read that story every year, I somehow missed this distinction between Christmas and Epiphany—that there is a significant amount of time between the birth of Christ and the arrival of the magi. Some say it may have taken years.

I love that some cultures build this wait time into their celebration. It seems to make the holiday—and the anticipation leading up to it—that much more significant. Such a tradition reminds us that every arrival is not an event, but a process. And I have a tendency to forget that.

So what does this talk of Christmas and gifts and magi have to do with you and me and how we spend our everyday lives waiting? I'm an adult now, and the glory of what December 25 once held has now faded. I no longer sit at the bottom of the basement stairs in the morning, awaiting the arrival of seven o'clock, my parents shouting down to tell me I can come up and see what Santa brought. But even now, I'm living in anticipation of good things to come—not just in the winter, but in all seasons. And now, after years of learning certain lessons about life, I realize the magic of Christmas was never about the day. always about the waiting.

Life is full of good things we haven't yet experienced: finding a spouse, having that first child, taking the long-awaited vacation after years of hard work. Retiring. Graduating. Becoming who we want to be. However, if we're not careful, we can rush through the process of living on our way toward the next anticipated arrival. We can waste hours and days and years looking at our watch, eager for the following appointment.

Our journey is full of rest stops—park benches and airport terminals—that signal the arrival of things we anticipate. Sometimes, they're worth the wait; other times, the glory doesn't shine quite like we'd hoped. Regardless, we need to learn to live in this tension, to appreciate what we have and still hope for. This process isn't easy; we all know that. But it's part of being human and it's what connects us to each other.

We are all waiting for something. And in that wait, there is a necessary tension, even a frustration, that doesn't fully resolve. This doesn't mean some things aren't worth waiting for. It just means we don't always get what we want, and rarely does it come all at once. Believe it or not, this is a good thing. Just like the delayed gratification between Christmas and Epiphany, we need to understand that the wait sometimes is essential to appreciate the gifts that follow, no matter how much we may resent the process. So through the angst and anticipation, in our longing to have and be more, we need to learn to enjoy this place.

CHAPTER FOUR
Calling

FROM MUSIC *to* WORDS

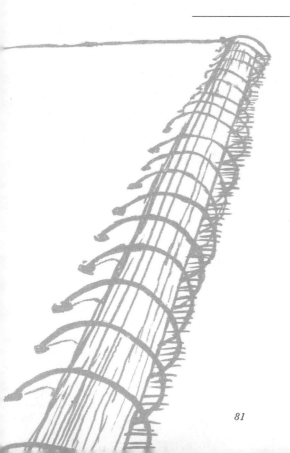

Sometimes, all we need to do to find our calling is to look at what we love and see what's always been there. The journey of discovering my life's work was not a process of dreaming but remembering.

I always thought I wanted to be a rock star. But the more I pursued music, the more I realized it wasn't right for me. My true vocation was hiding in the shadows, watching from afar like a distant love interest, always taken for granted.

That's the funny thing about a calling. Like the girl next door, it can sneak up on you.

Some people wait their whole lives for the right career to come along, refusing to begin their lives until they have more clarity. Longing for a vocation that will complete them, they sometimes never find their life's work. What I've discovered is that the opposite is true: while we wait for our callings to present themselves, they are waiting on us to wake up to the signs.

In high school, my dad bought me a used electric guitar by trading in my neglected tenor saxophone for a cheap Fender Strato caster knock-off. It was blue and came with a black gig bag, and I thought it was the coolest thing in the world.

That's when I decided to become a rock star.

In the early eighties, my dad played in a band called Majik. Back then, it was still cool to misspell common words and call it art. While I was growing up, he would regale me with stories of his time with the band, which included meeting Bob Dylan at a party and jamming with Neil Young's buddies. He even dated one of the girls from the band Heart. My dad—a working-class Joe with a tattoo of a wizard on his arm—was cool. A real rocker. And with him as my teacher, I was destined to be one, too.

After practicing playing guitar for six months without much improvement, I got frustrated. Able to limp through only a few simple songs, I wondered why I was no Carlos Santana. Did I just not have what it took? Angry, I took my complaint to my dad.

Snatching the guitar from my hands, he showed me how to play a barre chord by holding down all the strings with one finger. He told me I couldn't jump from one end of the guitar to the next, that I had to gradually work my way down the neck. And the same was true for playing solos. I had to practice.

Shortly after that, I started writing songs. I had always been a sucker for words, and with my music, my love for language had a new outlet.

Growing up, I watched the movie *Eddie and the Cruisers* with my dad more times than I can count. We saw it so many times on VHS that the tape slowed down and distorted the sound in certain places.

During one scene in the movie, Eddie, the lead singer, tells Frank, their lyricist: "Words and music, man. They need each other."[5]

As a new songwriter, I was beginning to discover how true that was.

Most nights in high school, I stayed up late, crafting poems that would someday have music behind them. Sophomore year, I found two guys who liked to jam, and together, we formed a band called Decaf. Determined to not be called copycats, my two new bandmates and I played almost all original music, which was rare for other bands we knew. We weren't a cover band; we were a real band with real songs. And I was the songwriter. Finally, I'd found my muse, a reason for living and creating. Or so I thought.

In college, I continued to play music. As I did, I became comfortable with writing songs. I joined a band that played music for our weekly chapel services, and we often formed side projects. On the weekends, we would travel, playing shows wherever anyone would have us. I was certain this was my destiny.

Around the same time, at the request of one of my professors, I started tutoring students at the Campus Writing Center. I wasn't an English major, but it was a way to make money using my familiarity with words. I certainly never thought it'd lead anywhere.

After college, opportunities to pursue music continued, but my passion waned. I toured the country with a band, playing more shows than I ever would have imagined. Other than sleeping or eating, music was all I did. As a result, I became better than I ever thought possible. Realizing I could now be as good as I wanted—it was really just a matter of practice—I was now faced with the dilemma of whether or not I wanted it. Playing gigs was no longer exciting, and I often felt distracted while playing guitar. Maybe it was the lull of life on the road, but I began to wonder if music really was my calling.

In between gigs, I started writing. Not having composed content longer than a song lyric, I decide to write a short story. The idea came while driving through the Midwest, surrounded by cornfields, with nothing to do but think. So I began.

Every night, while staying at a different place in the country, I wrote a piece of a story that I would email to myself so I could resume writing it at the next stop. At the end of the year, I presented the story to my then-girlfriend, Ashley. No one other than her will probably ever read it, but that's okay. There was something thrilling in the act of writing it, something freeing. An experience I wanted to have again.

That same year, I spent a few hours each week writing a report of the band's activity that I would then post on the Internet.

The following summer, despite my reservations, I started a blog. Having heard of this trend of online publishing, I thought at first it sounded stupid. Why would anyone care what I had to say? Despite my doubts, I tried it anyway. The experience gave me the same thrill as when when Ashley read my story. It was like playing a live show.

Around that time, my friend Dale, who was contemplating what he would do for the rest of his life, told me, "If I couldn't play music, I don't know what I'd do."

As I watched a group of musicians nod in unison to the wisdom of these words, my head remained fixed. I wondered what was wrong with me.

I'd just do something else, I thought.

Such a thought brought anxiety. Although I'd been playing guitar for seven years, I wasn't in love with it. This made me worry that maybe I'd missed my calling. Were all those years wasted?

A few months later, I chased Ashley down to Nashville and was hired by a nonprofit as a writer. This was the first time anyone called me a "writer." It would take years before I'd be willing to admit that to myself. My job with the organization was to help staff and volunteers tell their stories through blogging, a hobby I'd just started months before.

Upon receiving the assignment, I went to Borders to pull every blogging book off the shelf. There were five of them, and most included words and phrases I'd never heard of before. I was in over my head. But after a while of faking it, I finally figured out this craft of writing and publishing online.

A year later, my boss asked me to start a marketing team. Returning to the same bookstore to scour the shelves for another topic, I once again felt overwhelmed with the pressure of having to do something I'd never done before. But eventually, I got the hang of that job, too.

...ring the next four years, I hired writers and designers and ...; editors, sometimes pulling long days of work that left me with little energy to play guitar or do anything else creative. At that point, I had stopped writing. But even in my stillness, something stirred.

Once in a while on a Saturday afternoon, when the wind was blowing just right, a feeling would come over me, and I'd pick up my laptop to write—for hours. Crafting words about life and what I thought of the world, I wrote. Just to write. With no intent of ever getting published. The content came from a place deep in my soul where the things I make are made for love and nothing else.

At first, it was merely an escape, but eventually it grew into something more serious. After writing in private for months and then years, I was able to get a few stories published in some national magazines and on some popular websites.

More than once, my wife asked me, "When are you going to write a book?"

Laughing and shaking my head, I'd acknowledge her question and then return to my busyness, avoiding the answer. Years later, it was obvious that she wasn't asking. She was telling.

One morning, I picked up a book my wife had been reading and skimmed over a random page. The author wrote about how she became a writer, and the story resonated with me.

In music, you can hit a certain note and if it is the same frequency as a nearby object, the object will vibrate. This is why we see in old cartoons ladies singing opera and breaking windows. It can actually happen.

As this author struck her chord, describing feelings of guilt and shame as she first started writing, I felt something strange and energetic shake in my soul. She liked her day job but still wanted more; it did not fulfill her completely. During the day, the call to write distracted her, teasing her with promised satisfaction to come, like a love affair. A sense of shame for "cheating" on her occupation overcame her. As I read this, my heartbeat quickened, because I too, felt that same shame she described. It was a feeling of deceit or betrayal. Everything about wanting to be a writer felt wrong, so I suppressed it, buried it deep. It just felt too selfish, too wrong.[6]

A year later, a friend asked, "What's your dream?"

I rolled my eyes.

At the time, most people I knew were talking about their dreams, and it was starting to get old. Maybe they were bored or searching for a better job in a down economy, but I had enough to do. Instead of dreaming, why not just get a job? Did everyone really need to have a dream?

My thoughts betrayed my cynicism: "I don't have one." I was resolute in my declaration, then for flavor adding, "Actually, I'm living my dream right now."

The last five years, I'd submitted to someone else's dream, and had grown in so many ways as a result. Under the tutelage of my boss, I watched peers chase empty passions, ending their pursuits in frustration, while I learned how to be a steady apprentice.

Yes, this was the road less traveled. And I was better for taking it.

"Weird," my friend said, his voice taking on a therapeutic tone. "Because I would've guessed your dream was to be a writer."

At the end of that statement, his voice raised in tone, as if he were asking a question — but he wasn't. Something about the way he said "writer" struck me, like the word itself hit my soul with a resounding *thud*.

I swallowed hard.

"Well, I guess you're right. I would like to be a writer . . . someday."

He laughed and shook his head, sighing.

"Jeff, you don't have to *want* to be a writer. You *are* a writer. You just need to write."

My eyes enlarged in mystic wonder, pupils surely dilating. *Really? That's all it took?*

For years, I wrote and published some of my best work—and still, I didn't feel like a writer. I would tell people I was "someone who wrote," but not a writer. Never a writer. Just a guy with some words who occasionally got published. No big deal. But when my friend said those nine wonderful, weighty words—*you are a writer, you just need to write*—it felt as if a veil had been lifted from my eyes. I had seen the light.

So I began to write.

Having heard that serious writers get up at five in the morning, I started doing the same. Some mornings, I'd write three hundred words; other days, I'd write over a thousand. But none of that mattered. What mattered was I was getting up every day to pursue my passion, not for the sake of improvement or achievement, but for pure love of the craft.

The more I wrote, the better I got. Apparently, all those years blogging and teaching other writers hadn't been for naught. One day a friend said, "You've found your voice."

Maybe I had.

It had happened so gradually that I'd hardly taken notice. But like picking up the guitar one day to find it no longer hurt my fingers, I found a similar familiarity with putting my fingers to the keyboard. Maybe I was supposed to be a writer.

But then again, I'd been through these emotions before. How did I know this would stick, or that I was even good enough to make it?

Carrying these thoughts around with me, I responded t
old friend's invitation to meet up for coffee.

My friend Shane is the best guitar player you've never heard
of. I seriously believe he could hold his own with some of the
world's best: Steve Vai, Joe Walsh, even Jimmy Page. He's that
good. Like me, Shane spent a year on the road with a band. In
fact, he spent a *few* years traveling and playing music.

The difference between us was how we spent our free time
in between gigs. I spent those long hours on the road listening
to music, counting mile markers, and falling asleep. Shane did
something different: he practiced. Every spare moment he had,
he would pick up his guitar, crawl to the back of the van, and play
scales for hours, trying to get just a little bit better. I always admired that and wanted to know what drove him to such discipline.

When we got together for coffee, I asked Shane what he
thought about gifts and if people could be naturally good at something, like music or writing. Or, I wondered, did it just come down
to good, old-fashioned hard work?

"I teach kids all the time who think playing guitar is just something cool to do," he said. Shane has also been a music teacher
and tutor for many years. "They come in for maybe four or five
lessons, and then they're done. Once their fingers start hurting,
they give up. But—" he paused and leaned forward as if to share
a secret, "—every once in a while I meet some kid who has it. In
one lesson, he has learned what takes most students six months to
learn. And he just gets it. Sometimes, these kids have never picked
up a guitar before in their whole lives, but they totally get it. They
can *hear* what it's supposed to sound like. I don't know what you
call that, but that's a gift."

I nodded, feigning understanding, but honestly befuddled.

"So what do you do with the kids who aren't gifted? Do you tell them they don't have *it*?"

He shook his head. "I would never tell some kid who has an interest in music to quit, because I've seen kids work hard to play a few simple chords, and I see the look on their face when they've done something they didn't think they could do. I believe we all have natural inclinations—things that we just love doing. And we forget that's also a gift."

I nodded, trying to make sense of this. It was great to hear Shane talk of his passion for guitar, but I wondered about those who weren't as good and committed as he was. I wondered about folks like me who were fickle about so many things, even guitar. And what did this mean for my writing? Did I have "it"?

"If I were terrible at this," he said, "I'd still have to do it. It's something I feel *called* to do. God never promised me I would be successful at guitar; He just called me to do it—so I want to do it well."

My eyes lifted from the crêpe I was devouring and locked with Shane's. I knew exactly what he was talking about. Yes, *calling*. Ever since I sat down to write a story about gargoyles in sixth grade, I had sensed that same feeling—the compulsion—he described. It was the need to create, to make something you were proud of, even if nobody noticed or acknowledged your effort.

Shane wasn't born playing music. He wasn't like Beethoven, picking up his instrument before he could eat solid foods. He started playing guitar in high school when his youth pastor encouraged him to play in the church band. Quickly, he found himself loving it, setting aside all his free time to practice. Who knows if he had a natural gift before picking up the guitar? But what's certain is that he loves to play. So he does it as much as he can and has done so for years—not because someone forced him to but because the craft deserved it.

When I began to write more seriously, to really consider myself a writer and act like it, I felt a call to write as much as I could. To practice. Not for the sake of getting better, but out of respect for the writing itself. I couldn't avoid it any longer; it was a compulsion that consumed me.

Steven Pressfield says that in pursuit of our life's work, we often chase shadow careers. These are things that look like our calling, but aren't.[7] This can be an addiction, another hobby, or just plain old procrastination. As I started writing, I could see how everything I'd done up until that point was prologue, preparation for the main event. The sixth grade spelling bee I'd won. The fascination with songwriting. Even the year on the road. These were all shadows of something to come. Mile markers on the highway to my calling.

A calling, as my friend Clint says, is "something you can't not do." It's a driving desire, a prompting at your back or side that doesn't relent until you give in, until you answer. Until you finally surrender. That's why our life's work is more than a dream; it's a calling. It calls to you.

I've always had a way with words. Or perhaps, they've had a way with me, tracking me down and calling me back to the work I was made for. For a long time, I took this for granted, didn't appreciate it. But now I understand. This journey was never about success or arriving; it was about obedience.

While I played guitar, I was overly concerned with my insufficiencies. Not being the next Jimi Hendrix meant utter failure. Insecure and embarrassed of my own inabilities, I was often beating myself up for not being good enough. Now as a writer, I try not to think like that. Maybe because I've put down the guitar and picked up the pen, exchanging a desire to look a certain way for coming to grips with my purpose.

These days, I spend my free time writing—not because I want to be the best writer in the world or receive accolades from fans, but because it's something I can't not do. It's something that must be done, regardless of skill or reward. I try to do my best, but being bad isn't a good enough reason to not try.

Such conviction didn't come as an epiphany, with flashing lights from heaven and the booming voice of God. It came as I understand many people's callings come: quietly. In a space where I was on my way to be one thing and instead became another.

When this happens, the call can be subtle, as a simple realization of what we ought to be doing with the rest of our lives. This is what compels us to climb into the backseat of a van to practice playing scales for eight hours or endure the discomfort of a soggy, wooden reed placed between our lips. It's what calls us to work past the pain of carpal tunnel and overcome obstacles of being whatever it is we say we ought to be.

Some say a calling comes from a muse or the work itself, but I believe God is the one who calls. Like most things from the divine, a calling is hard to describe.

Oswald Chambers says, "If you can tell me where you got the call . . . I question whether you have ever had a call."[8] A calling is mysterious, but those who have been prompted know it. Unsure of the location or exactly what I was doing when called, I look back on life and realize there were many moments in which it was clear I was supposed to be a writer.

In a way, this is something I've been waiting to do my whole life, unwittingly preparing and practicing for years. That's what it means to find a calling. You don't actually find it; you become it.

Through this process of stepping into one's life's work, once again we learn to wait. We wait for a dream to become a reality. For a passion to turn into skill. For us to be ready for what God has for us next.

Perhaps the hardest part of realizing my calling was how easy it was to ignore. I could, after all, have continued working at my day job without ever needing a new challenge and would have kept being congratulated for my work. But I would have deprived myself and probably others of something important, something significant. Maybe what I write won't ever make an impact on anyone but me. And if that's the case, I'm fine with that because I am doing what is mine to do, and that's all any of us can really hope for.

Not everyone finds their calling. Certainly, it's not something we have to do; it's a choice, which may be the scariest part. If you and I aren't paying attention to our lives—if we don't possess the patience to examine our gifts and talents—then we just might miss what we were made to do.

Maybe that's the point of the in-between. All things we wait for are not merely roadblocks on the long journey; they are the journey. And each stop has a crucial lesson. In other words, it wasn't enough for me to become a writer; I had to become the writer who traveled and played music and learned the importance of working through the delays of life, so that I could become the person I was meant to be. And maybe that's what we all need: not to accomplish an arbitrary list of goals or pursue a plan already laid out, but to find the one that's waiting for us, that's been there all along.

IN-BETWEEN GLIMPSES

Only being twenty-six, the phrase I've heard for many years goes something like "you have plenty of time to gain experience." That was all good and well, but they didn't know what I knew. I mean, I'm a fairly smart person with a level head on my shoulders. But everyone else seemed to think I needed to "wait" to move forward. Wait to apply for a higher-level job. Wait to write a book. Wait to speak on "that" topic. Wait to get married. Wait to have kids. Wait, wait, wait. What "wait" meant to me then was, "We don't think you know anything."

Now, I can look back and see what they mean. More time simply means more experiences. More time allows for more reflection—on not just the silly things I've done, but the smart things as well. Now, I'm able to approach things better than I did a few years ago. I've spent time networking, reading, listening, working, thinking, and praying. All of this helped me realize what the wait meant—time developing me.

—Miranda

CHAPTER FIVE

Courtship

LOVE *takes* TIME

As long as I can remember, I've never liked the idea of marriage. Maybe it was seeing my parents have a hard go at it or the number of friends I knew who grew up in broken homes. I don't know. It just seemed like a failed experiment, like something people made too big a deal of, and I wanted no part in it.

When I went to college, the decision was cemented. After a hard end to a long relationship, I decided to swear off the whole institution entirely. I half-joked with a Catholic friend on his way to the priesthood that I'd just join him and become a monk myself.

I was afraid. Afraid of making the same mistakes I'd seen others make. Afraid to fail. And maybe afraid to love someone else who might hurt me. All those fears changed, though—one summer that never should have happened.

I wasn't waiting to fall in love, but I fell in love while I was waiting.

During my senior year of college, I lived in a houseful of women. The building was school property with separate living quarters, and four Spanish-major students were allowed to live in it. It just so happened that those four students were three girls and one guy—me. Every time I share this story with another guy who's never lived with girls, I get a high five. But anytime I share it with a man who's grown up in a house full of sisters or raised his fair share of daughters, I get a different kind of reaction: an empathetic sigh and shaking of the head. My senior year of college was more the latter than the former.

That year, I found every excuse to avoid women—not only those living in my house, but also those living on campus. After a year-and-a-half-long roller coaster of breaking up and getting back together with the same girl four different times, I'd sworn off dating. And just to be safe, I was keeping my emotional distance from females in general. I stopped flirting (okay, I didn't stop entirely) and grew bitter toward the farce formerly known as "love." I even made my friend Paul promise me that if I got too close to a girl, he'd call me on it. It was my last year of college, and I wasn't about to be distracted by girls. I had dreams of exploring the world, and those dreams did not include female companions. These were solo dreams. Bachelor dreams. My dreams.

A few weeks before the summer started, I received a phone call from Ashley, an acquaintance I'd met earlier that year and barely knew. She was putting on a party and needed a sous chef. Always eager to flip a few burgers, I told her I'd be happy to help.

Ashley was athletic — a softball player in high school and a dancer in college. She was a commuter and had a polished look of sophistication most students who attended class in their pajamas lack. She wasn't short, but neither was she tall. Her long, brown hair went past her shoulders and had a few blonde highlights, signaling she was ready for summer. I didn't know her well, but what I did know was that she was fun and full of energy and always game for a good prank. What little I knew of her, I liked.

A few days after I agreed to help with the party, the phone rang. It was Ashley again, wanting to know if I'd go to the supermarket with her to pick up the food. We set a time to meet and then proceeded to stay on the phone for another twenty minutes. After hanging up, I paused, considering what had just happened. I left my room confused.

"I think Ashley Cooney just flirted with me," I said.

The party went well. The burgers were delicious, the games a hit, and everyone had a great time. After going home for the evening, I realized I'd forgotten my sweatshirt back at the party and returned to find it missing.

A few hours later, Ashley called, telling me she had the sweatshirt. I jokingly accused her of stealing it and demanded she return it immediately. Really, though, I was just looking for an excuse to see her again. That night, we talked for over an hour on my front porch. By the time we said goodbye, I'd forgotten all about the sweatshirt.

After that, Ashley and I stayed in touch. We learned we both were staying in town after graduation, so it made sense to be friends. We got into the habit of teasing and playing pranks on each other, and I suppose what I was really doing was flirting back. But I never would have admitted it. After all, I'd sworn off girls.

In May, my roommates left, and the college gave me permission to stay in the Spanish House—with the addition of a male roommate. *Good,* I thought. I was ready for some "guy time." I didn't have a job or a car and had few prospects for employment, but I had a place to live. A place that was finally female-free. And that was a start, a beginning to the monk life I sometimes seriously longed for.

By the time summer came, I'd already made my commitment for the following year. Excited for a year of travel ahead of me, I couldn't wait to begin. I didn't want to be there in Jacksonville, Illinois, that summer, but I definitely didn't want to be anywhere else—not home and definitely not at school. It wasn't time to be anywhere else, much less where I longed to be, which was out on the open road. All I could do was wait.

Before I could spend a year out on the road, I had to raise funds for my living expenses. So I started the summer writing letters, asking people for money. One of those people was our church's worship leader, Richard. Richard was about my dad's age and had a similar taste in music: the Beatles, Grateful Dead, and Bob Dylan. He had round, John Lennon–style glasses, some stubble around his mouth, and a receding hairline. Every Sunday at church was a Lynyrd Skynyrd reunion, and I was often tempted to shout "Free Bird!" from the pews.

One day after church, Richard pulled me aside and told me he was having some work done on his home. Since he knew I was looking for work—and trying to raise money—he gave my name to his contractor, Tim.

I worked in carpentry that summer—my first time swinging a hammer and wearing work boots. The job meant long days, but I didn't mind. The weather was perfect that summer in Illinois, and I was finally learning to become a man. I packed my lunch every day, keeping it cool in a small, red Igloo cooler. Around noon, I would get a twenty-minute break, and I'd often pull out my parents' cell phone, which I rarely used, and call my friend Ashley. I wasn't planning on befriending any girls that summer, but when all my guy friends moved away, I didn't have a choice.

I had only four friends that summer: Jared (my roommate), Curtis, Abby, and Ashley. When everyone from college moved away, the five of us stayed. Every night, we'd get together to play games, watch movies, or share a meal. In a way, it felt like family. I rarely thought of Ashley and Abby as *girls*; they were more like sisters to me. Abby was a tomboy from Michigan who was tougher than I was, and Ashley was—well—just different.

In July, when the corn grows high and the heat of the Midwest finally rises, summer emotions start to stir. Curtis and Abby started dating, which only drove Ashley and me closer together. Not necessarily romantically, just out of necessity. With those two spending all their time together, our circle of friends quickly shrunk. When Ashley's birthday approached, I decided to throw her a party. At that point, I never would have admitted I liked this girl, but I wouldn't have denied wanting to be closer to her. There were, of course, deeper motives astir.

So my friends and I threw her a party, a really great one. It was a luau with tiki torches and Hawaiian shirts and even a kiddie pool full of soft drinks. With the help of some friends, I went all out, and frankly the gesture surprised even myself. I'd never done such a thing for a girl before, but I just felt that she deserved it.

I stayed late that night and was one of the last people to leave. She thanked me for the party, and I said something sarcastic to her, and that was that.

About a week later, Ashley and I went for a walk, as we sometimes did. We were so bored that summer that sometimes she'd just come over to hang out, but this was not one of those nights. Since the party, I'd been thinking about telling her how I had started developing feelings for her. But I didn't know how to do it. I thought a walk might make it easier.

We ended up at the football field where Ashley used to dance during halftime. Without a blanket, we lay down in the grass to look at the stars—not touching, of course—and she started telling me her dreams. She told me of her hopes, things I'd never heard her say before. She talked about her aspirations to travel and experience the world, about the adventures ahead of her—all things I wanted for myself. But I had been sure Ashley didn't want such things. Without any prompting or provocation, she was telling me how she wasn't content with her job and was even considering going on a mission trip next summer. That was when everything changed.

Immediately, I recalled a conversation I'd had with myself a few months before. It was right after the "stolen" sweatshirt incident, when I admitted for a moment I had feelings for this girl. For a lot of reasons, that moment scared me, and I wondered what such feelings meant for me and my future. *Was this a distraction or a new direction? Should I acknowledge these thoughts and feelings . . . or ignore them?* I decided to repress them, believing this was absolutely the worst time to begin a relationship, as I was about to leave for a year.

But the more Ashley shared that night about what she wanted out of life, the more my heart raced. Although it was a beautiful, balmy summer night, I began to sweat. *What is happening here? Does this mean what I think it means? Why am I all of a sudden so nervous?* This conversation was so random, I had to assume this was the sign I'd been waiting for. Which meant I needed to act.

During a lull in the conversation, I stared up at the sky, the stars just beginning to come out, and taking a deep breath, I said four important words:

"So here's the deal . . ."

Turning away from the sky to face Ashley, I saw her soft hazel eyes and her brown bangs hanging over her face, and I thought she'd never looked so beautiful. But maybe I was just starting to see what had always been there. I told her that although I was leaving, I wanted to commit to her. I said I knew it would be hard and wasn't even totally sure what that meant—to commit. In two weeks, I'd be leaving—we both knew this. And not just for a month or a semester, but an entire year. We knew there was risk and a high possibility of failure, but we also knew in the magic of that moment that this was something special, something that deserved our sacrifice.

Without knowing what we were heading into, we decided to go for it. Although I had no idea how hard it would be, I felt it was right. And in that moment, all I knew was something significant had just happened.

Rising from where I'd been lying on the ground, I extended my hand to Ashley, offering to help her up. As my hand grasped hers and I helped her to her feet, I didn't let go. We started walking home along the newly paved sidewalk of an old neighborhood, each too shy to look at the other.

Two weeks later, I left. The night before my departure, my dad drove downstate to get my things. We loaded up his pickup truck and the next morning drove back to Waterman, the place I'd called home for eight years before leaving for college. A week later, I went to Minnesota to begin my year of travel.

Ashley and I agreed to write letters. The wait would be long—eleven months apart before being able to actually date each other. It was a good, old-fashioned courtship, an antiquated arrangement that not everyone understood. But we knew what it meant: we were waiting for each other. And somehow, we flourished during those times when we could have failed, in between that first date and the time we would live in the same zip code again. With letters and late-night phone calls, with trust and faith and the belief that a two-week relationship could turn into a life-long love—we made it work.

After that year apart, we both moved to Tennessee in the fall. Ashley got a job in Nashville, first working a temp job and eventually getting hired by a record label. I slept on a friend's couch and worked a couple of part-time jobs. The wait was over, but we were about to face a new in-between time.

This next season of our relationship was difficult. We were used to sustaining a long-distance relationship, not maintaining one in which we got to see each other every day. The long-anticipated proximity to each other was actually quite a challenge. There were even a few moments in which I wondered if we'd made the right choice, if the relationship would indeed endure.

But in May, I bought an engagement ring.

"It'll burn a hole in your pocket," my friend Dustin told me. He was right.

One night, three weeks after purchasing the ring, I couldn't sleep. Overcome with anxiety, I stayed up until three in the morning, writing a song—actually, rewriting one. *Our* song: "Hold On." I'd written it for our first date, played it for her on a park bench in Jacksonville, a week after we first held hands and a week before I left for a year. It seemed appropriate.

Just before four, I drove to Ashley's apartment. Arriving outside the complex, I snuck in by following someone through the gate. In the woods right outside her place, I spread a plaid blanket on the ground and tried to keep warm. For May in Tennessee, the air was unusually chilly, and my hooded sweatshirt wasn't doing the job. I pulled out my cell phone to check the time. Still a few minutes before the sun would come up. I had to wait.

Glancing up at the sky, I saw the last star fade as the morning light grew. The sounds of car engines starting signaled the beginning of a new day. I reached into the pocket of my hoodie to touch the thing that had haunted my dreams. The ring. The engagement ring. Something I never thought I'd own. Wrapping my fingers around the round golden object, I pulled it out of my pocket as if it might explode. I didn't know much about jewelry before this, but now I knew exactly what a solitaire with a "princess cut" diamond looked like. I was holding it in my hands—the setting was small and square, modest but beautiful. I'd spent most of my savings on this sign of commitment, and in a moment, I was going to do something I never thought I'd do: ask a girl to marry me.

Having left the box back at home, I tied the ring to the drawstring of my sweatshirt and dropped it down my shirt, letting the cold metal rest against my chest. Saying a quick prayer and shivering from the cold, I pulled out my phone: 4:58 a.m. Close enough.

I dialed the familiar ten digits, and after a few rings Ashley answered. I gave her precise directions, ones that I'd rehearsed in my mind on the twenty-minute drive in between my apartment and hers: *go outside, follow the music, don't ask questions.*

She complied.

Meeting me on the blanket, my girlfriend sat cross-legged, glaring at me with sleepy but suspicious eyes. Without saying anything, I began playing the guitar. At first, I avoided her gaze, but by the last verse, our eyes had locked. And at the end of the last chorus, I sang the words, "Will you marry me?" Her eyes grew wide, and I had to look away. This was it.

Finishing the song, I set the guitar down in the dirt and rose to my knees. Without cue, Ashley joined me. No longer shivering, I now had little beads of sweat forming on my forehead. My heart was racing; fear gripped my soul.

I could still decide to not do this . . . right? No. I wanted to do this.

Grasping the string on my sweatshirt, I pulled out the ring, and she gasped.

"Wow." A puff of fog escaped from Ashley's lips. My insecurity evaporated, as did the fear and anxiety. I told her I loved her and asked if she would be my wife. Together, both on our knees, the smell of wet wool rising from the morning dew, we pledged our lives to each other. In the remainder of twilight, we sat beneath the sky, our whispers getting lost in the sounds of the rustling leaves and people beginning their days. We stayed there together for an hour. Then Ashley had to go to work, and I took a nap.

Following this moment of wonder was eight months of worry. As the wait ensued, old fears and concerns assailed me. I loved this woman, but would marriage ruin that? Was this the right time to give my life away to another person? Would there ever be a right time? I'd seen so many friends abruptly break off engagements or have their marriages ravaged by infidelity. I had no delusions; I knew marriage was dangerous. I was hopeful we could be different, but at the same time skeptical.

Months after I proposed to Ashley, reality set in. It's not like I was having second thoughts, I just knew marriage changes people—makes them stubborn, selfish, and sometimes even mean. I didn't want that for us. Still, I believed in a hopeful alternative; I just needed to see it.

"Marriage is hard," I told my pastor, Ron, during one of our weekly meetings many months before the wedding date. Slouching in the seat across from his desk, I looked at the books on his shelf behind him. We'd been meeting like this for over a year now, ever since I'd moved to Nashville and started attending the church down the street from my apartment.

"I've not found that to be the case," he said, and I raised an eyebrow. "I know some people say that," he continued, "but it's not been true in my experience. I *love* being married."

I didn't know what to say. Was he serious? Growing up, this was a bedrock of my beliefs about the institution of matrimony. It was the reason I assumed I'd never get married, why I was now struggling with this idea of commitment. Marriage was hard—for everyone. And way too hard for me to undertake. *Parents fight, kids get yelled at, and stuff gets broken.* This is the way it was. If you could survive this failed institution without a divorce or any major scars, you were one of the lucky ones. In my mind, stepping into holy matrimony was the same as stepping on the battlefield: it wasn't safe, and there was no guarantee you'd make it out alive; but most people appreciated the sacrifice you were making.

Now Ron was messing all that up for me.

That day we ended our meeting sooner than usual, and afterward I kept thinking about what he said. What did he mean marriage didn't have to be hard? I had to admit he looked pretty happy with his wife. But how could he say such a thing with so much certainty? I wanted it to be true for Ashley and me, but still I had my doubts.

The following week, I drove from Tennessee to Georgia for a work trip. I stayed with my friend Mark, who is twice my age, and the kind of guy who makes you feel immediately at home with him. He's also so smart that he could easily make most people look stupid, but instead, you leave his house usually feeling better about yourself. Or at least, I do. One night during my stay with Mark, we sat outside on his deck by the pool. And he asked if I was excited about getting married.

"Well . . . sure," I said. "I can't wait to marry Ashley, but . . . I dunno. I guess I don't expect much to change. A wedding just seems like a formality to me, you know? I've never really been that into ceremonies. I don't think it'll be a big deal. Just another day, right?" I tried my best to sound intelligent and hide the fear I was feeling. I needed someone else to justify my cynicism.

Mark looked at me, his eyes narrowing as if in deep thought. He paused and then responded, "Well, I don't know about that." His tone was calm and collected; he always thought about things before saying them, unlike me who often blurted out whatever I was feeling. Then he added, "My wedding day was the best day of my life."

I turned to him, waiting for the punch line. It never came. He was completely serious. *The best day of his life? For real?* I waited for something more, some jab at the institution of marriage or gripe about his wife, but he just let the words linger. They seemed to float toward me and sit on my shoulders, like a dad resting his hand on his son's back. For a while, neither of us said anything. We just sat in the dark, beneath the moonlight, with the crickets to keep us company.

Mark's words stirred a vision in me. I yearned for something more from my marriage than what I'd seen or heard about growing up. And I started to believe that if it was possible for Mark and Pastor Ron, then maybe it was possible for me, too.

Ashley and I finally got married in January. The day turned unseasonably warm, with temperatures in the seventies by the time the ceremony commenced. We ponied up what little cash we had to pay for the wedding and coerced our friends into helping us with the setup and preparations, making handmade decorations and borrowing lights and chairs from the church. Everything from the cutting of the cake to the pouring of the punch had been delegated, and if one person didn't do his job, it all would have fallen apart. These small but seemingly critical concerns only magnified my overall worry, because there was a lot riding on this day for me. A lot more than whether or not a cake got cut.

When the time for the wedding march arrived, our pianist didn't play Pachelbel's "Canon in D" as we'd rehearsed the night before. In fact, she didn't play at all. Instead, my best man, Dustin, left his place on the stage and, despite my protests, sauntered over to the stool we had set out for him. He picked up the guitar and sat down. My palms started to sweat, and I looked at Pastor Ron with pleading eyes, begging him to do something, but he only returned my glare with a smile. This wasn't supposed to happen until later in the ceremony. But now the doors were opening and everyone was standing and it was too late. Here it was: the mishap I was dreading, the sure sign of worse things to come. If the wedding was a catastrophe, surely the marriage would be worse.

But as soon as I heard Dustin strum those first three notes, as soon as I saw Ashley emerge from the lobby, I knew what was happening. It was the song. That song. *Our* song. The one I'd played for Ashley on our first date. The same one I used to ask her to marry me. She'd sent the words and music to Dustin to learn, and now she was walking down the aisle to it. As all my friends and family rose to watch my bride make her march, I joined them, tears rolling down my cheeks. Behind my back, she'd performed this most beautiful of deceptions.

Watching my wife-to-be walk toward me, while hearing my own words of promise and commitment sung back to me, I started crying. And I didn't stop. Not for the vows. Not for the message. Not even for the rampant applause when the "You may now kiss the bride," came. Anyone who was there will tell you I was a blubbering mess; I could barely choke out my vows. All because of a silly little song—but not just any song on any day. Our song on *our* day. A surprise that spoke volumes about what this commitment meant to Ashley—and was beginning to mean to me.

That's when I understood. As the song ended and my bride drew near, I began to believe. I believed in marriage, whether it was wonderful or hard, whether we would struggle or wake up to endless days of joy—or maybe all of the above. I understood how my parents could get separated, divorced, and then remarried to each other years later, how it wasn't about having a perfect story but one that endures. I believed in what I could never see before. I believed in this person who believed in me, in this woman I was waiting for.

Yes, I cried that day like no man wants to be reminded of, and all my friends do, anyway. It was a day full of grace and love—too much for one person to take in. Too much for a single day, for one unseasonably warm day in January. It was a day I thought would be "no big deal," but looking back, I can see how wrong I was. Without a doubt, it was the best day of my life, one I continue to learn from.

The past five years of marriage have been full of ups and downs in between that day and this one. We've had our share of frustrations and mishaps that have shaken our faith a time or two. But we are stronger and better for the challenges we've faced. And we continue to believe and hope for good things to come.

Since that day, my wife has stood by my side at every major moment, the victorious along with the disastrous. She's been my biggest fan and helped me anticipate good things when I tend to be cynical. Because, as we've both learned, sometimes life surprises you. My wedding day is a good reminder of that.

The unexpected path to marriage that seemed like one long line of inconveniences was far less accidental than I thought. What felt like months and years of waiting were, in fact, preparation. This in-between time helped me understand what it means to commit, to love without condition or reservation. And when the day came, I was ready.

Sometimes, the best gifts in life are the ones you have to wait for.

Hold On

by Jeff Goins

Hold on to me, girl
Hold on to what you never believed
Hold on to me, girl
'Cause this could be,
This could be—
Real.

IN-BETWEEN GLIMPSES

I knew I was about to miss my connecting flight in Denver. The flight attendant let me off the plane first, and I still didn't make it. The airline put me up in a hotel. The shuttle bus left at 10:30 p.m. for a forty-five-minute ride to the hotel. I had not eaten any dinner, and I was hungry and tired. The flight the next morning was at 7:00 a.m., which meant I had to catch the morning shuttle back to the airport at 4:45 a.m. The guy beside me on the 10:30 p.m. shuttle said, "Well, nothing we can do to change things now. We may as well relax and breathe deeply." That's just what I did. I said to myself, "Relax, it is what it is."

—Don

CHAPTER SIX
Expecting

THE PATH *to* PARENTHOOD

She's pregnant, finishing her first trimester. It's Sunday morning. We slept through both church services. Or rather, she did—on my lap for a couple of hours while I read a book. For a moment she protests, insisting we can't miss another service. I don't even entertain the idea, as I can see the exhaustion in her eyes. She rests her head on the pillow on my lap and closes her eyes.

The hours effortlessly pass us by—Ashley in her dreams and me in my book.

I've finished reading now, but I can't bear stirring her. Even when my legs fall asleep, I don't move.

I wake her slowly, and she sits up, still groggy. The pregnancy has done this to her: made her sleepy and easily exhaustible.

It's eleven o'clock in the morning and she's hungry. I ask my wife if she wants anything to eat, but nothing sounds good. We are both used to this drill by now.

Eggs? She gives me a cross look.

Leftovers? She mumbles something about eating Mexican in the morning. Sounds like a no, but the rationale baffles me.

Pancakes? She nods approvingly. She never says no to pancakes.

I smile and get right to work. Pouring a huge glob of vegetable oil into the pan, I turn the burner dial to "5." I'm still getting used to the electric stove, still getting used to our new home with its new gadgets. The pan heats up, and using a paper towel, I wipe out the excess oil. Today is one of the many days we don't have Pam—but we always have pancake mix.

With a ladle, I pour two circles of batter into the pan. I decide to look for the spatula; why I do it in this order, I'll never know, but this reckless process happens more often than I'd care to admit. Opening the door to the dishwasher, I move around some utensils—nothing. I shut it. Pulling out drawers and slamming cupboards, I frantically search for anything that will flip. My quest quickly ends in futility.

This is our new house, full of new things. And I can find nothing.

Air bubbles begin to form along the edges of the first two cakes. "That's when you need to flip them," my mom used to tell me.

Yes, I know. But with what?

Another look through the dishwasher yields the same results as the last. Now I'm actually nervous, and I pull out drawers, check under the sink, pace back and forth—from kitchen to breakfast nook back to kitchen again. Still, nothing. Calling to Ashley in the next room, I ask if she knows where it is.

"I have no idea," she calls back in a sleepy voice. I can barely hear her over the exhaust fans and wonder if she went back to sleep. Desperate, I grab a wooden spoon I bought at the Dollar Store. It's for rice, I think. It'll have to do.

Attempting to scrape two crusty cakes from the sticky part of the old nonstick pan, I sigh. They won't budge. Somehow, I am able to force them over in the worst flip of pancaking history. The cakes make it to the other side, but they are mangled beyond repair. The first batch is always bad, right?

I'm a messy cook, but that's the beauty of pancakes: you expect loss. It's part of the process. You're making something wonderful, and what feels like waste is just how it works. As I scrape the cakes into the garbage, I start again.

This time, I leave more oil in the pan but don't yet pour the batter. Opening the dishwasher a third time, I rummage around with a little more patience this time. And there it is. That stupid spatula—buried beneath several plates and bowls. I emit a half-sigh, half-chuckle.

The next batch is perfect. With spatula in hand, I watch intently and with pride; I am now ready. No pacing, no frantic searching. The bubbles form, and some steam rises. Even with fans whirring, a wonderful smell fills my nostrils and then the room.

Ah, yes. This is what I was waiting for.

When they're done, I stick the cakes in the microwave to keep them warm. I continue this process for fifteen minutes. Pour, flip, smell, smile. There's a wonderful rhythm to it. I am in my element, finally in control of some small part of my life. And that's a rare occasion these days, as I prepare to be a dad.

When the final batch is finished, I remove the pancakes from the microwave and replace them with a plastic bottle half-full of syrup. As the molasseslike substance warms, I lather each cake with butter in preparation for what's to come. Then, I pour the gooey mass of maple on top. Finally, finished.

After a laborious process of friction and frustration, I look around the kitchen. It's a mess, a battlefield of chaos and triumph. Drops of batter cover the countertop—would-be pancakes fallen in the fight. A little smoke fills the air, and there is a sink full of pots, pans, and last night's dinner dishes. All reminders of the busyness and craziness that consume more and more of our days.

I've been cooking pancakes my whole life. I'm pretty good at it, too. But each time is like the first time. It never ceases to amaze me how messy it can be, how sloppy I am. Every time, I relearn that creation cannot come without sacrifice—even if it's just a mess in the kitchen.

Before we take the first bite, Ashley and I look at each other. I wink, she grins. No words are exchanged. None are needed. And I wonder, as we quietly lift our forks to our mouths: *Will we ever have mornings like this again?*

It's February, months before the day when we welcome our son into the world, and my wife and I are eating at an Irish pub at the Opryland Hotel in Nashville. Normally, we'd never be able to afford a room in a place like this, so when I got the invitation to speak at a conference here, I asked for one.

When the waiter delivers our bangers and mash, I raise my glass and offer a toast to Ashley: "To Aiden," I say, confidently proclaiming the name of our unborn child for the first time.

For weeks, we've talked about this, ever since we found out we were having a boy. The name appealed to me, but only in theory, when I assumed we were having a girl. I've needed some time to decide if I really like it. For a while, indecision plagued me; I was unsure of committing, afraid of the permanence of settling on a name. But soon our son will be here, whether I'm ready or not, and I'm beginning to resign myself to the fact.

After thinking about and imagining what it'll be like to teach my boy to be a boy—and one day, a man—the name has grown on me. It's an Irish name, so it'll match his inevitably light complexion and probable red hair. He's not even born yet, and I'm quite certain he'll favor my looks. The name literally means "little fire" in Gaelic and is the namesake of an Irish saint known for his missionary work during the Dark Ages.

Yes, I think. *He will bring light to the dark.*

He already has.

My wife's eyes grow wide at my declaration, and she asks, "Are you *sure?*" She knows how fickle I've been about this, how indecisive I can be. She's waited for me to settle on a name that seems right and good. This name was her idea, even the atypical spelling, so she doesn't want to force it on me. I give her my nod of approval that says the discussion is done. So she smiles and raises her glass to join me.

"To Aiden."

And with that, we wait for new life to come.

"We're going to have to tear that baby out of you right now." That's what the doctor might as well have said at our thirty-five-week checkup.

We're at the hospital for the follow-up appointment to check our baby's heart. This is our second visit. Our unborn son has a heart arrhythmia, but we're told this is nothing to be alarmed about. Still, we're nervous.

This must be what it's like to become a parent, I think, *beginning the journey of worry and obsession over a child's health.*

The blips and blops on the monitor screen are confusing, but the doctor deciphers them in his best attempt at layperson's English. He fails. As we listen to the monitor, we hear the beats run in perfect rhythm for five, maybe ten seconds. For a moment, I think it's gone. And then . . . there it is: a slight syncopation.

Blip, blip.

Blip, blip—

—Blip.

That's it. The arrhythmia. The break in the beat. If his heart were an orchestra, we would notice. It would feel wrong, incomplete. But we're told this is nothing to worry about, something that often corrects itself at birth. They tell us the trauma of birth helps, but I can't imagine how something traumatic can lead to good. The doctor insists we visit him every week up until birth—an event over a month away.

We finish our visit.

After the doctor exits, the ultrasound technician stays to clean Ashley's stomach with a cloth. She wipes off the last glob of whatever fluid they use in ultrasounds, and I help my wife to her feet. As we exit the room, we remember we wanted to know how big he is. Ashley asks the nurse, since they forgot to say during the ultrasound. The woman returns to the monitor screen and says he's about five pounds. Then she stops and out of her mouth comes the scariest sound a soon-to-be-parent can hear:

"Oh."

Oh? What does she mean, "Oh"?

"It looks like his stomach is a couple of weeks behind . . ."

Then she asks the other ultrasound technician to get the doctor. And for a moment, nobody says anything. Ashley and I stand there, not daring to look at each other.

I should say something . . . but what?

A moment later, the other tech returns with the doctor who looks at the screen and frowns. Then he says that same terrible word, the word I can no longer stand hearing: "Oh." There is a space in those two letters, an awful incompleteness that leads you to too many terrible conclusions. In that moment, I feel excluded from an elite club of medical professionals especially fond of vowels.

"See that?" the nurse asks. He nods. The doctor asks us to sit down, and he uses some device — I think it's called a Doppler — to check the flow of blood to the baby through the umbilical cord. Then his mouth opens and out comes a series of words we don't understand. Our dumbstruck looks don't seem to faze him, as he continues soliloquizing in spite of our puzzled looks. We try to follow along, pretending to have medical degrees, because it all sounds so important and serious. I want this talk of placentas to make sense to me, but it doesn't; and by the end of the doctor's discourse, I am even more confused.

All I understand is something about how few nutrients are getting to our baby, which explains his small stomach. This has nothing to do with the heart arrhythmia; that's just what alerted us to these other issues. They're quite confident the arrhythmia will correct itself at birth.

I turn to my wife, expectantly. She's always been better at understanding these types of things, or maybe she's just a better listener. Yes, that's it. She pays better attention to these sorts of things, and I rely on her for it. But I really tried this time and still didn't understand. I'm just hoping she got what I could not. Her look of worry confirms my hope, but in the worst way possible.

These past eight months, I've counted on my wife for her intuition, that special knowing that maybe all mothers have. It's a secret knowledge that helps in critical decision-making mode, guiding you when you don't know what to do. When it came to picking out a crib or what color to paint the nursery, Ashley always had the answer. She just knew. But now, neither of has the answer or knows what to do; even intuition fails us.

Finally, after all his ramblings, the doctor says something we *do* understand: "This baby will have to come out." We must look stunned, because he clarifies with five more words that bring it all home for me: "You'll be parents by tomorrow."

In a matter of moments, we have to grow up. Or rather, I do. Ashley's been ready for this for a while. I can see it in the calm in her eyes. But not me—I've been procrastinating. Until now, it's all been an idea, an imaginary game that might someday be reality. I was hoping to make the most of the wait, and I planned on having one more month to prepare to be a dad, but now that's all gone. Today, the game goes away. Today, we become parents. And I learn that some things you do not get to wait for; you do not get to bide your time until you are ready. Some things you only become when you must.

After a call to the obstetrician and a quick trip to her office, which is only a floor below us, we're checked into the hospital.

The next five hours are a blur. I run to the car to throw to-gether a makeshift "go bag." This includes freebies from a recent baby shower that were stowed away in our backseat. I toss them all into a mesh, green grocery bag and present it to Ashley, proud of my accomplishment. She is now lying in bed and doesn't have the heart to tell me I've just brought her a bag of useless stuff: three-month-sized onesies and diapers too large for a tiny baby. But I already know. I'm just trying to keep myself busy, terrified of sitting still and keeping quiet. I must keep moving; otherwise, I'd have to admit how little control I actually have of the situation.

Using Ashley's cell phone, I call her boss and HR department, requesting that her medical leave begin immediately.

"Tomorrow," I say. And then I have to repeat it. "Uh-huh. We're gonna have a baby tonight." I can't believe the words I'm saying. All of this is a surprise. We thought we had all the time in the world, but instead, these final moments of anticipation are filled with the worst kind of fear. The kind where we don't know what might happen next.

Next, I call family. First Ashley's, then mine. My mother-in-law, who lives seven hours away and is every bit a planner, tells me, "Okay, we're on our way." I am shocked at how calm and collected she sounds. For the next hour, though, she is a frantic mess, hurling bags into the van and rushing to get out of town as quickly as possible. My parents, who live closer, tell me they'll be at the hospital in a couple of hours—as soon as our son is born.

Eventually, I run out of people to text, email, or call, and all that's left to do is wait.

At nine o'clock in the evening, Ashley goes into the operating room, and I wait outside in my blue scrubs, hot breath fogging up my new glasses. I bought these plastic-rimmed glasses only a few months ago, because I thought they made me look hip. Funny, I don't feel hip right now. In fact, I'm embarrassed now at how much I care about things like looking hip, things that don't matter—because in this moment I truly understand what does. As I sit in a hard plastic chair with an uncomfortable back in the hallway outside the room where my son will be born, my heart is racing. I am waiting to become a dad.

I think of a lyric from a Death Cab for Cutie song, which offers a strange comfort: *And it came to me then that every plan is a tiny prayer to Father Time.*[9]

Yes. That's what I'm doing here: praying. With my thoughts and apprehensions, I grasp for something steady to hold on to. I pray our son will be healthy and that everything will be all right. I try to remember the Lord's Prayer or the Twenty-third Psalm, even the Serenity Prayer, anything to ease the worry. I barter with God, even though I'm pretty sure He's not the gambling type. I make any deal I can to ensure everything will be fine and everyone I care most about will be okay in the morning. I force out incomplete sentences, hoping divine ears can intuit what I mean by, "Help . . . please . . . "

Then I sit. And I wait. And I have no more words.

Moments later—or maybe hours, for all I know—a nurse exits the OR and tells me I can come in. They set me beside my wife, and all I can see is her face. They won't let me stand up. If I could, I'm not sure I'd want to. This is the moment we've both been dreading. They told us our baby was so small his lungs might not work. If we hear him cry when they pull him from the womb, we'll know he's okay. We'll be able to hold him, and he won't have to go somewhere else—someplace where they help babies learn to breathe. I don't know much about such places, but I don't want my son to have to go there.

Ashley asks when they'll start cutting into her. She has been petrified of a moment like this her whole life. When she was younger, she had a bad experience in which the anesthesia for another operation didn't take, and this is the last place she wants the drugs to stop working. Her one concern and worry throughout the pregnancy has been the pain. She doesn't want it to hurt, doesn't want to feel what she doesn't need to feel.

The nurse chuckles. "Hon', we've been working for about five minutes now." My wife lets out a sigh, and I reach out to find her hand, the only appendage I can grasp on this side of the blue cloth acting as a screen between us and our son.

As the suction tools start sucking, and the doctors operate on my wife, I whisper a thousand prayers. I've never been this afraid, never needed faith so much. The not knowing is killing me; I want to stand up and see. At this point, seeing something, anything, would be better than the waiting, the guessing and the wondering. But they won't let me; I have to wait until the doctors finish. As they do, the dreaded moment arrives. We hear bits and pieces of conversation and a hundred thousand dollars' worth of medical supplies at work— unfamiliar noises in an unfamiliar place.

"See that, there?"

Slurp, slurp.

"Yep."

Whizzzzz . . .

"Oh, there's an arm!"

Rrrrrrrrr . . . Schwoop!

"Look at him there. A little guy, isn't he?"

The voices and sounds coalesce into a cacophony of buzzing, whirring, and dialoguing over the machines. At this point, I'm holding Ashley's hand, squeezing hard and hoping the medicine is working. The last thing I want is for her to feel the pain of my nervous vice grip. From the sound of it, our baby is out of the womb, but we hear nothing. This is the moment we worried about, the one we were so afraid of.

According to the doctors, delivering prematurely is the right choice. If we had continued with the pregnancy, he may have suffered from a lack of proper nutrients and blood. But delivering a baby a month before his due date is not without complication. He could experience all kinds of problems, including the inability to breathe properly. Given the two potential outcomes and their respective risks, choosing an early delivery seemed the safer solution. At this point, dealing with such complications would be easier outside of the womb. It's the smarter risk to take. That's what they tell us.

As the doctors remove my baby from my wife's belly, my heart seems to stop for a moment, ceasing all pumping of blood to vital parts of my body. I hold my breath, wondering what this next moment might mean for us. In the interminable silence, which may have only lasted a second or two, I think my worst thoughts and worry my worst fears — ones that always come in the darkness of not knowing. The fears all parents are well acquainted with. Again, I pray — this time for a few simple tears from him. Never again will I want a sob so badly as right now.

Just one cry, I think. *That's all I'm asking for.*

And then it's over. An instantly familiar noise follows: the cry of a baby. My baby. Our perfectly healthy boy. Someone laughs as he pees across the room, and the tension lightens.

For the next hour, I hold his hand and cry over him, thanking God for those wonderful tears. He never goes to the NICU, but instead, spends that first night of many to come with his parents who love him.

It's late, and I'm tired. Again, our newborn son is stirring. He's only ten weeks old now. His body is still small, well below what he should be weighing, what he would've weighed had he been born on time. He recently started sleeping more during the night, but not this night. Tonight, he has other plans.

Ashley has finished feeding him and just passed the boy to me. It's my job to burp, change, and put him back to sleep.

I get right to work. As I pat the baby on the back, waiting for a loud, raucous sound to escape his tiny mouth, he starts to cry. After several minutes of patting and bouncing, it becomes apparent he's not going to burp. I cradle him and try rocking him back to sleep. He won't have it. He keeps crying, and I grow anxious, worried I won't be going back to sleep anytime soon. It's been nearly two months since I've had a decent night's sleep. I used to pull all-nighters in college, but this is different. I'm older and the sleep deprivation is beginning to wear on me.

The cry has turned into a wail and now—a scream. I pull myself out of bed, resigned to the fact that this little boy is not going back to bed without a fight. I'm already exhausted from the previous night's episode. I can't remember what happened then; all I know is I'm tired.

My eyes half-open, I swaddle our son in the dark, wrapping him in thin sheets we bought at Target for more than a glorified blanket should cost. But eventually, we broke down, deciding no amount of money was too great for a few hours of uninterrupted sleep. Pulling the cloths together tightly and tucking them in around his arms, I secure my son in his very own mummy wrap. He continues crying.

I bounce him and rock him and sway back and forth, singing softly to him as I do. I am a slot machine of baby-bouncing techniques, hoping one of these motions will work—believing something has to soothe him back to sleep. Still, my son cries.

I go to the rocking chair and sing another song. I read him a book. Then I swing him softly in my arms, even lay him on my knee and bounce him. Nothing works. His sobs are becoming un-controllable; and he is becoming more and more agitated, nearly inconsolable.

Finally, I give up. I surrender to the fact that tonight is an-other night when I'm not going to get any sleep. I change my expectations, preparing to be up until morning. I pick up my son, walk downstairs—careful not to stumble in the dark—and slump down in the couch. I unwrap him and instead of laying him down on my lap, I sit him upright like a big boy. I think about turning on the TV but resist the urge. For a moment, we sit there on the couch together, father and son, side by side. I look at him and smile, grateful for this new life that has cost me so much, but also given so much.

And slowly, his sobs start to subside. He opens his eyes, a few teardrops lingering on his cheeks, and looks around. At me. At the couch. At the canvas portrait of his mom and me behind us. I turn him around to face me. He's much more awake than I am; he smiles, then giggles at me. His eyes are wide with wonder, and I start to bounce him on my knee, using one hand to hold his head up. He goos and gahs at me.

We do this for a while, maybe thirty minutes—although, I'm not exactly sure, as we seem trapped in another reality, somewhere in between dreams and waking. He doesn't tire, and neither do I.

After an hour of play, I finally lay my son down on the couch, and for the first time that night, he is still and silent, staring at the enormous universe of our living room. Everything is new and wonderful in those eyes. As I watch him exploring his surround-ings, I join him in appreciating the moment.

Eventually, we drift off to sleep together. But before I give in to unconsciousness, a thought comes to mind. I consider what would have happened if I hadn't taken the time to come downstairs and tend to my son. If I hadn't surrendered my sleep to experience this wonder, I never would have had this moment. We never would've laughed together; I never would've seen his smile. Sure, there would have been others, but not *that* smile. In those wee hours, I discovered the joy of slowing down to live at the speed of my son.

As I fall asleep, I whisper a thank-you to the space that accompanies the gap between evening and morning, a divine space. A place in which I am certain God is.

I've dedicated countless hours to rocking and patting and bouncing my son to sleep, hours I can never get back. I've lost them. Looking at my child resting peacefully after our sweet exchange, I realize that if I *could* get those hours back, I wouldn't want them, anyway.

IN-BETWEEN GLIMPSES

I remember waiting for potential work to come in when my husband first opened his flooring and construction business—and no customers were to be found. I worked part-time as a florist to help make ends meet, but we both wanted me to stay home with our children. Instead of letting the financial strain and stress destroy our marriage and family, we made the best of things until our plans worked out. After a few years of hard work and humility, my husband's business provided enough for me to stay home. I feel like a better mom and wife after having to endure such a difficult time.

—Shar

part three

WHEN *the*
WAITING ENDS

Several months ago, I called my old college buddy Paul. We talked for over an hour on the phone; the main topic of discussion was where we'd ended up and how our lives were different than expected.

"I just turned thirty," Paul said, "and *that* was weird."

"Yeah . . . why?" I asked.

"Well, there were just a lot of things I thought I would have done by now."

He proceeded to list a handful of accomplishments he thought would be completed. You have to understand something about my friend Paul: he's an overachiever. He was the guy all the professors were talking about when he graduated, saying to each other, "I wonder what he's going to end up doing!" The world was his oyster, and he was going to make something of himself.

So now that Paul lives in a small town in rural Minnesota, working for a grass-roots nonprofit organization, it's easy to wonder, "What went wrong?" But that would be missing the point.

At age thirty, Paul thought he would have finished grad school by now and be teaching at some university. But he hasn't done any of that.

"And that's okay," Paul said. Then he added, "I guess." He said it wistfully, a twinge of doubt in his voice. My friend may not be living up to the expectations of his anticipated professions, but he is, however, married, quite happy, and handy with a snowplow. In that conversation, though, I wondered if all of that was enough for Paul. It was hard to believe he meant what he said about it being "okay."

As the conversation continued, Paul went on to tell me everything he'd done since college, like training hundreds of musicians every year to travel around the world and play music for tens of thousands of people (the touring bands we were both in). He described how his life had changed since meeting his wife and how he could make changes to the ministry he was working for.

He said it was hard to come to grips with the fact that all his dreams hadn't come true. I admitted I'd felt a similar feeling at times, wondering if I'd ever be able to be content with life.

"You know, Paul," I said, experiencing a minor epiphany, "life hasn't turned out the way I thought it would, either. But I wonder if the proper response isn't, 'Oh, God . . .' but rather, '*Thank* God.'"

Sometimes, the hardest times are the ones when the waiting never seems to end. For a friend to finally get clean. For a wayward child to return home. For a healing that never comes. For the future you thought you were going to get.

Unfortunately, life is full of times like these in which there is no resolution. The pain never seems to make sense and the confusion never goes away. These fuzzy times are full of frustration; these, perhaps, are the moments in which our patience is tested the most. But disappointment contains its own clever lessons; it has a surprising moral to teach us, if we will listen. If we will pay attention to the signs.

Sure, we struggle with making sense of this life, of understanding why Dad had to leave when we were so young or why we could never shed those final fifteen pounds. We long for the homecoming that never happens here on earth, and if we're not careful, we could very well end up regretting and resenting this whole existence.

And we would be missing the point.

The word "disappointment" comes from the idea of literally missing an appointment. It originally was used in the context of meetings and gatherings. If you disappointed someone, it meant you told someone you were going to do something and then didn't keep your word. So what does it mean if we are disappointed with life? Did life make a promise to us that it didn't keep? Did she promise to always meet our expectations or to keep us comfortable? Can we really be angry with God that things don't turn out exactly the way we thought?

A few weeks ago, I saw Paul over Thanksgiving—we were both visiting family and in-laws—and he told me that he finally believed that even though life didn't turn out the way he planned, it turned out better. He told me Minnesota was now his home. And something occurred to me. Maybe our disappointments aren't missed appointments at all.

Maybe they're calls to patience, or simply signs of a change to come. When we lose a dream, it may be more than loss. As in the case of Paul, it may be a gain of something we never expected or understood. So perhaps the fact that life doesn't always turn out the way we'd hoped is a blessing, not a curse—if we have eyes to see it.

CHAPTER SEVEN
Bookshelves

WHERE *old* STORIES END

I'm sixteen years old. It's early afternoon. And despite sun pouring in through the windows, the room seems dimly lit. I know this room. There's a bathroom off to the side where I took my first shower—a rite of passage for a boy used to bubble baths. My mom stayed here after having my sister. I also stayed here while she was in the hospital; I read a letter from her every day that she was gone. All in this room. It's a place of beginnings, this room. But not today. Not this drab, dreary afternoon.

The priest recites words from a book that is not the Bible. They are practically inaudible. Even if I could hear them, I would not understand. How could I? Looking around, fidgety, I sigh. I am bored. Around me are bookshelves lined with works about famous authors whose names I don't yet recognize—but I will, someday. Dostoevsky. Hemingway. Stein. There are biographies, bibliographies, and literary analyses. It's an appropriate place for a journalist, a caretaker of others' stories, to die.

In the corner of the room rests an oil painting: an abstract piece with illegible words bleeding into distorted faces. It's disturbing but beautiful. At the bottom of the canvas is the inscription: *CS Ward*. Charles Seaman Ward—my grandfather.

This room is a microcosm of his life—a story of a story. Did he long to live a scene from *A Farewell to Arms* and regret not fighting his own fight? It was his health that kept him from the war, but he supported it, nonetheless. Was it enough to paint like Picasso in private and play jazz for his grandkids, or did he hunger for more than facsimiles of an admired life?

I can't help but think of regret and feel guilty for sometimes dreading coming to this house. It was often messy, which was stressful for my mom who owned a cleaning business at one point. There were always books and stacks of newspapers lying around, loose-leafs of sheet music to be found on any table in any given room. They were, in a way, pictures of my grandparents' life, but they were memories for my mother, some of which she'd rather not remember.

We, his family, sit around him. The priest continues, but Grandpa and I lock eyes. His face is yellow, jaundiced, and hard to look at. This is not the man I knew. He has no novel near him, no article clippings or anything to read. Where is his book? I almost grab one off the shelf and place it on his chest just to make him—or maybe me—feel more at ease. Instead, I place my hand in his soft, piano-playing hands. His grip is surprisingly firm for a musician, a man I always knew to be a delicate diabetic, wincing whenever I walked near his feet.

The priest asks, "Do you repent of your sins, Charles?" Tears fill Grandpa's eyes. Nobody called him Charles. Like Charlie Brown to Peppermint Patty, he was always, "Chuck."

When the priest asks this, I wonder what memories come to mind. Family vacations to South Haven? Years of drinking and yelling? The time he confronted Dad—a kid with long hair and a tattoo—telling him to get out of his house? Maybe none of these. Maybe all. Or maybe any number of other dark secrets too dangerous to touch the pages of his many journals, some of which surround us on these very shelves.

It must've been Grandpa's passion for journaling that rubbed off on my mom, and it was certainly her obsession for recording life's events that influenced my own diary keeping. Now as I watch this final scene unfold, I try to take it all in, remembering this moment in case it never meets the page of a journal.

Grandpa nods in response to the priest's question. My eyes begin to burn and liquid salt pours down my cheeks. The priest continues. And we all watch; unchurched people we are, but still keenly aware of the sacredness of this moment.

"And do you receive Jesus Christ, the Son of the Living God, as your Savior?"

Oh great, I think. *Here comes the religion . . .*

Watching in wonder, I'm curious as to how Grandpa will respond. Had he ever been to church? An avid bibliophile, he must've had a few Bibles in the house. But I don't recall him ever reading one, or even talking about God for that matter. On Sundays, Grandma went to mass, and he watched Matlock; that's just the way it had always been.

As we listen to the gospel, I wonder, *Does he understand this? Do I?*

Dad and I have been talking about this lately, and between the two of us, we think we've got God figured out. Dad was raised a Southern Baptist, and I've been to enough churches to understand a thing or two. Going to church is good and God is definitely real; He should be a part of your life, if you have the time. But we also believe there is a line that you do not cross when it comes to religion. If you do, there's no going back; you become what my parents call a "Jesus freak" — a hypocrite and a liar and someone who is just plain weird. Jesus freaks need powerful prayers of confession and earth-shattering epiphanies, while the rest of us can rely on common sense and social convention. No, we do not believe being too religious is a good thing. Nor do we think a person's life can change in an instant.

But at that moment, I wonder if we've been mistaken.

As these thoughts bounce around in my brain, Grandpa looks up at me from bed and smiles. Seeing the warmth in his eyes, I return the smile, trying to be present to what's transpiring before me. He turns back to the priest.

"Yes."

The word is robust, brimming with conviction. Surprised at the sudden surge of my grandfather's strength, my eyes are now wide; I am no longer bored.

"I do."

Turning from the priest back to me, Grandpa squeezes my hand. And once again, he smiles.

As a farmhand from Iowa, my grandfather was no stranger to struggle. While studying writing at Reed College, he worked at a shipyard in Portland. But he did what he could to provide a better future for his children. He read and studied and landed a job as a journalist. A cultured man with a passion for theater, Charles Ward pursued the arts in all aspects of life. He wrote plays and films and acted on stage; he published articles and interviews and even helped make a film. Although he came from humble beginnings, he was smart and accomplished. So I wonder what use of spiritual things he had—even now, on his deathbed.

Here in this room, surrounded by my grandfather's closest companions—his books—while classical music plays on a stereo somewhere, I am puzzled at his sudden transformation. I knew he was brilliant, and I admired this man and almost always respected his idiosyncrasies. But I never took him for a sucker, never thought him to be someone who still believed in fairy tales.

Despite my cynicism, I watch as Grandpa prays with the priest, and I can tell something significant is happening. He is changing. I can feel it in how he clenches my hand, his gaze locked on mine. Why now? I wonder. After lots of physical pain and even the death of his eldest son, why does he turn to God now—after so much trauma? Is the fear of death enough to scare him into righteousness? Or is it the weight of life that has finally worn him down?

Whatever is happening right now, I know it is real.

For a moment, I forget about the diabetes and grumpiness, the sugar-free Jell-O and Saturdays on that worn and dated couch; I let go of the awkward exchanges at Christmas and having to constantly repeat myself when he says "What?" while cupping his ear. I even excuse the monotony of watching another episode of *The Andy Griffith Show*. I forget for a second that my grandfather is dying.

And I think of this man—the playwright and poet, pianist and painter—and I want to tell him everything.

I want to tell him who I will become and what I will do. Want to make him proud. I want Grandpa to know I will go to college and star in plays, that I will play music and learn to love jazz like he does. I will listen to public radio and enjoy it. I want to tell him I'll write news pieces and magazine articles; that I'll become a book snob, obsessed with first editions and hardcovers—just like him.

I want to tell him that I'll pray that same prayer he just did—someday.

But I can't. Because I don't know these things yet. I am only sixteen years old. I must wait many years before I will understand. Instead, I say through sniffles, "Love you, Grandpa." He says he loves me too. Even without dentures, it's clear.

And that's it. No more words. No prayers. Just my grandfather surrounded by the books he loved in that unforgettable room. And then we leave.

On the drive home, my dad attempts to explain death to me, to help me understand how it's a part of life. But I don't want to be comforted. I don't want to know he's "going to a better place." What I want is to understand what just changed Grandpa, what made him pray that prayer—and mean it.

I think he waited his whole life for that moment. Little did he know, it would leave an impression for years to come.

───────────────

It's winter, but you wouldn't know it here in Taiwan where the only thing separating the seasons is the rain. It didn't rain today. Not yet, anyway—thankfully. This is the season for it. Some days, we don't leave the apartment due to the downpour. Even the moments of sunshine are somewhat bleak, a cruel reminder that this moment won't last long, that more precipitation is coming.

Our band—the group I've been traveling all year through North America with—has been here for a few weeks now. We'll be here through the end of the month, playing live shows on the streets of Danshui, a city outside of Taipei.

It's November now; we missed Thanksgiving. But there's plenty to be grateful for here, when we choose to recognize it.

Today, we loaded up our van and drove to a senior citizen center, somewhere out in the country. When we arrive, we enter bearing our instruments, ready to play. Our translator, Sandra, tells us to set down the guitars for a moment. She tells us what these people want isn't music but massages. Their muscles ache and joints hurt, and they long for just a few moments of physical comfort.

We begin by rubbing the necks and backs of those old enough to be our grandparents' parents. As uncomfortable as this makes me, I do it anyway, placing my hands on the shoulders of a man who must be at least ninety. He shudders when I do, squirming at first and then leaning back, relaxed.

When we signed up for this year of travel and service, my six companions and I surrendered our expectations. We let go of what we thought this adventure might look like, submitting to whatever the journey might throw at us. And although we've only been traveling for a few months, that's long enough to expect a few surprises.

After performing my third massage, someone asks us to share a word of encouragement. Our translator elects me, probably because I'm the leader, and everyone seems to agree. They want me to preach.

These people don't speak Mandarin — they're too old for that. Sandra tells me they only speak Taiwanese, the native language of the land now belonging to the Republic of China. She'll have to translate my English to Mandarin, and Jack, our driver, will translate to Taiwanese. I begin to speak, waiting three times as long for my two translators to relay the message to each other and then to my audience of about a hundred Taiwanese seniors.

Here, I feel fragile. These people are three times my age. What do I have to say to them? What cultural references can I share that they'll understand? Not only does an entire ocean separate our cultures, but there is more than a couple of generations between us. Flummoxed, I share the only story that comes to mind, the only one that seems appropriate in this moment. I tell them about Grandpa.

I explain how years ago I watched him die, and though I admired the man, I knew there was a darkness and emptiness to his life I couldn't explain. How I watched on his deathbed as he pleaded with God for forgiveness. How I watched his demeanor change in a matter of seconds. Too young to appreciate what was happening, I had still understood it was important. I'm a cynic about these things, I tell them, but this was the real deal.

Jack stops and looks at Sandra who turns to me with a frown, whispering, "Real deal?"

"True," I say, correcting my colloquialism.

That satisfies my two translators, so I continue. I explain how life is full of surprises; we never know which day may be our last.

"But there's good news," I say. "Every day we're given is a gift, and while there is still breath in our lungs, it's never too late to right a wrong or find forgiveness."

I encourage them to do what my grandfather did, to be bold and brave and honest with themselves. And I repeat: "It's never too late."

My fifteen-minute speech has turned into a forty-five-minute homily, thanks to the translation challenge. At the end, Sandra encourages me to ask if people want prayer. Never one to want to force religion on anyone, I apprehensively do, suggesting people raise their hands. Several do, and we surround the dozen or so people with arms held high. Whispering quiet prayers in our native tongues, we ask God that these people might find peace.

We encourage them to say their own prayers, to talk to God directly, telling them He understands all languages. Some of them ask for forgiveness, and a few even ask to pray that same prayer my grandfather did, so that they can know God like Grandpa did.

After the massages and prayers, we play a few songs. And then it's time to go. We pack up what we've brought—a couple of acoustics and a djembe drum—and head back to Danshui. By this time, it's raining, and we get wet while moving our gear to the van.

On the drive home, I think of Grandpa and what he prayed. And finally, I think I understand. I'm beginning to realize how our lives are comprised of both individual epiphanies and ongoing evolutions. Change doesn't happen in a moment, nor does it always come slowly over time. It's happening here and now, every day, in the big and small. And every moment is a chance to choose.

To not only accept the grace in front of us, but to boldly change the course we've been on for so very long.

I once heard a preacher use a term called "prevenient grace," which sounded like a ten-dollar word reserved for seminarians and scholars. But now, it has a new meaning. Sometimes, the transformation we've been waiting for is actually waiting for us, slowly drawing us in over time. Until one day, we break down or give in or simply decide to live differently. As I look back on the past few years of my life, I can see how that was happening in my life. What connected the moment on my grandfather's deathbed to that moment in Taiwan was years of in-between. And they were not so random or ruined as I once thought.

When we get back to the apartment, everyone goes to their respective rooms. Since the rest of the afternoon's schedule is empty, I walk over to the bookshelf full of old paperbacks and used books. I pull a title off the shelf, one I haven't read in years. Peeling back the cover, I start with the dedication:

> I wrote this story for you . . . You are already too old for fairy tales, and by the time it is printed and bound you will be older still. But some day you will be old enough to start reading fairy tales again. You can then take it down from some upper shelf, dust it, and tell me what you think of it. —C. S. Lewis[10]

I never believed in magic, never believed people could change in an instant or that miracles could happen. But then I saw one myself. I witnessed my grandfather change his life moments before he died, and I wondered what that might mean for me. Years later, I found a faith in something bigger than me, a conviction in goodness that was greater than my skepticism.

I always thought stuff like that only happened in the movies. Never believing the televangelists or slick-haired preachers, I was too smart for those sales pitches. But then one day, I saw change happen unexpectedly to one of the smartest men I've ever known.

And just like that, I began to believe in fairy tales again.

IN-BETWEEN GLIMPSES

I had to wait over two years for a diagnosis of my movement disorder. In the process, I lost the ability to do many ordinary activities. For example, my husband had to shave my underarms because my hands were too weak to control the razor. He didn't always want to do it, so I also had to wait for him to agree to help. Through these experiences I gained a much greater appreciation for the simple things in life; I also learned to empathize more with disabled people. All this helped me in caring for my mother and my stepfather during their illnesses and subsequent deaths.

—Brenda

CHAPTER EIGHT
Ice Cream

WHAT *really* MATTERS

We expected them to die two years before they did.

During our first few years of marriage, Ashley and I attended a small church in Franklin, Tennessee. The congregation consisted of about thirty people, and along with another young couple, my wife and I represented the twentysomething demographic. This was the same church we were married in, where we learned what it meant to be part of a community. Since we were both far away from home, these people became family. This church was the place where we were always loved—another home for us.

One year, we as a church buried two of our oldest members: Lois and Al. Within months these two pillars of our community were gone, leaving those of us who were left to wonder what it meant. It was a hard year. But just before each of these two left us, they taught me a lesson about life and death and what to do with the moments in between.

In the spring, we buried Lois, the matriarch of our church. Sassy but sweet, she lived a simple and inspiring life. With an infectious laugh, she had an edge that made her both fun and unpredictable—you never knew what kind of response you might provoke in Lois. It wasn't uncommon for her to razz you, even from the comfort of her electric wheelchair with a tank of oxygen trailing behind her—a comical image that was also part of her charm.

Lois was spry and jovial, even as her body weakened.

She left us gently and gracefully but with flair that was uniquely hers. At the funeral, her son-in-law, Vince, eulogized her, telling stories of his mother-in-law's love for antics. He recounted how she gave him a hard time while he was courting her daughter, and how he learned to give it back. The first night they had him over for dinner, she asked, "What do you like to do for fun, Vince?" expecting him to say music or hiking or something similar. Having been informed of her knack for teasing people, he said with a straight face, "Kissing. I like kissing." The whole table erupted into laughter, and from that moment on, Lois loved Vince.

As I listened in the funeral home, I laughed through tears and looked around the room, wondering how many others were recalling their own experiences. I was thinking of the woman I knew who always welcomed me with an ear-to-ear grin, followed by a greeting in her unmistakable Virginian accent. Even if she did so from across the room, Lois never seemed to miss an opportunity to smile.

When the family went to the beach together on vacation, Vince told me, Lois would leave rubber snakes under people's pillows and hide them in their top drawers. "She loved to laugh and tease," he recalled, "but did so in a very kind and loving way. . . . She loved life." *What an inspiration*, I thought. Of course, I'd seen this myself, but in bits and pieces and mostly from afar. So when Pastor Ron, her other son-in-law, asked me to carry Lois's casket, I accepted. Part of me wanted to be closer to her and this life that she'd led.

In the early afternoon on a Wednesday, we drove down Highway 100, past Music Row and the busyness of Nashville, to the place we would bury Lois. The motorcade led us beyond the Natchez Trace and the Loveless Café, each turn of the road sending me farther away from civilization. Looking at the clock on my car's dashboard, I started to sweat. I'd have to turn around at any moment to go to the airport and pick up my in-laws who were flying in that day to stay with us for a few days. I had overbooked myself—too many commitments and not enough time. But I kept going. I had to see how this story ended.

For forty minutes, we drove through the countryside of West Nashville, under low-hanging trees and along creek beds, the city turning to suburbs and suburbs turning to empty, barren fields. It was hot and dry that spring, and we were expecting a drought that summer. As we crossed a river, driving over a bridge, I wondered if we'd passed into another state—maybe Arkansas or Alabama or Mississippi. It seemed like we'd been driving forever.

As we drove that endless stretch from funeral home to cemetery, I thought about this woman we'd soon bury. Having met her shortly after we joined the church, it took me months to understand and even appreciate when she was teasing me. Each time I saw Lois, whether at church on Sunday or a community meal on Wednesday or a party on Saturday, she was beaming. Even through plastic tubes protruding from her nose, her visage shone. People say a certain person can light up a room, and usually it's hyperbole; but in Lois's case, it was true.

One Easter, Ashley and I went over to Lois's house after church. We ate lunch with the family—her husband, daughters, sons-in-law, and granddaughters—as if we had always been a part of the group. Even though we'd never been there, it felt familiar, like going to Grandma's house for a holiday. I don't recall what we discussed, but I remember hearing Lois's intermittent laugh throughout the conversation and seeing that unmistakable smile from across the table as someone passed the deviled eggs.

By the time we arrived at the gravesite, the sun was resting high in the nearly clear sky, puffy white clouds filling the vacuous blue. The midday sun beat down on our backs, causing the men who carried the casket to break into an immediate sweat as soon as we lifted up on the cold, metal handles. Our two-piece black suits were no match for the Tennessee sun.

The day we buried Lois, Ron shifted roles from son-in-law to pastor. With open Bible in hand, he read us the Scriptures and spoke briefly about comfort and grief. The verses he read reminded us that death was the "last enemy" and would one day be defeated, comforting those who had once grieved. As he read, the words coming from his mouth were slow and clear, articulate as always, but when he arrived at the section about enemies being defeated, he raised his voice as a sword in battle. And for a moment I thought I heard him shift back to son-in-law:

"But," he said, his voice strong and clear, "death is *still* an enemy . . ."

Yes, one day every tear will be wiped away and all things sad will be swallowed up, but until that day, what do we do? How do we process death and grieve the loss of what and whom we hold so dear? Is it okay to feel heartache, to hurt and mourn for the things we miss? Ron said this was not how it was supposed to be; we weren't made for such pain; this was a byproduct of living in a broken world that drastically steered away from how things were originally intended. One day, he assured, there would be no more pain, no more death. No more tears on a hot spring day. But until then, we had each other and the comfort of knowing some losses cause even a heart as big as God's to grieve.

Huddled around the casket as we watched it descend into the dirt, my worry of picking up in-laws vanished. For a second, I thought of Lois's smile, and I missed it. How do you not miss a light that shines so brightly? Nobody said a word as the long wooden box disappeared in the darkness of the earth. Offering platitudes seemed disingenuous and superficial, an affront to the life this woman lived. What Ron had said was perfect: *death is still an enemy*. On that dreadful day in April, when most of the world was being reborn, it felt for a moment as if this enemy had won. But as I looked around at the swollen red faces—some from the heat and others from the tears—I saw the beauty in the pain. In the company of those who loved this woman and were loved by her, I found the consolation of community. Though she was gone, we were still here, and we had each other; and maybe that was enough. Death had not won. For us, the sting of the wound was fresh, but Lois, as usual, enjoyed the last laugh.

Pastor Ron once told me a story of Lois and her husband Jim leaving town for a spur-of-the-moment fishing trip to Virginia Beach. Lois, whose health was starting to decline, wanted to enjoy what she loved most maybe one last time.

One morning before dawn, they stopped at a gas station. As Jim stood at the pump, filling up the RV, the man at the adjacent pump said, "Wow! I bet it costs a fortune to fill up that thing, especially in *this* economy!"

Watching the dollars tick by on the pump, Jim shrugged. Then he looked at the man to say, "I suppose. But my wife's health hasn't been that great, and she wants to go on a trip. So we're going." That was it, done deal. Didn't matter how much it cost or what they had to sacrifice — they were going to enjoy the last remaining morsels of life they could share together. And enjoy them they did.

This was how Lois and her husband Jim lived their lives. And this is their legacy — their loving sacrifice for one another and their endless example for people like me.

Lois had loved everyone like family. And maybe without realizing it, she became a sort of surrogate grandma to me. A grandmother is not always someone with whom you have the closest relationship — at least, not in my family. She is someone sweet and loving, gracious and kind — regardless of how rotten you are. A grandmother is someone who sends you cards on your birthday and gives you money for getting good grades on your report card. But other than that, you may not see her very much; you may not understand or appreciate the role she plays in your life, but she's there, nonetheless, assuring you that all is still right in the world.

Most of all, a grandmother delights in those whom she loves, regardless of whether or not that love is reciprocated.

For a brief but significant period in my life, Lois filled such a space. Away from the familiarity of home and family, I found a woman who had but a few moments of life left to live and spent some of them loving me, sharing her life with anyone she could. I didn't know her well—not as well as I would have liked—but she loved me, anyway.

We don't get to choose how many days of life we have left, but we can choose how we spend them. Lois taught me that. She was the one who by her very presence reminded us there was still good in this world and, maybe, in me. Through her steadfast spirit and constant love, she showed me the goodness even in the worst of circumstances. In her, I saw something I wanted—something bold and beautiful that demanded the most of every moment life was willing to give.

A few months later at church, Pastor Ron announced that Al had left us earlier that morning. At ninety years old, he had lived a full life, but his passing was still jarring to me. Another staple in our community—gone. What would I do?

As with Lois, I knew Al for only a season. He greeted me at the door when I first visited the church—shook my hand, showed me around, and invited me to stay for supper. He became my friend. Though we weren't related, it's hard *not* to think of such a warm, loving man as a grandfather.

Friends tell me the Al I knew wasn't the same man they knew. This Italian-American man was brilliant and brave—a soldier and engineer, an imaginative inventor, and a wonderful storyteller. He was someone who greeted new visitors as they entered the church. Though kind and gentle, he would cut right to the chase after shaking their hands: "Do you know Jesus?" he'd ask. Raised in Miami and Southern California, he learned Spanish (after his native Italian) before learning English. A member of the greatest generation, he fought in World War II, and though I'm sure the scars of war were still real to him, he was able to remain a gentle, sensitive man afterward. Later in life, he and his wife, Madelyn, taught English as a second language to Latin Americans living in Franklin. When he found out I had studied in Spain, he started speaking to me in Spanish. A hard worker and servant, he retiled the church's bathroom floor on his hands and knees when he was seventy. Pastor Ron, who was a few decades behind Al in age, said he couldn't keep up with him.

I didn't know that active, energetic Al. But the man I knew was all I had, and he was worth remembering. Maybe it was the fact that he didn't grow up with much money or maybe he just liked looking good, but Al was a precise, clean-cut man. Whenever he stood up, he would comb his hair with his hand and tuck in any renegade pieces of clothing that had fallen out of line. His short, dark hair was always straight and slicked down, his ironed shirts tucked into perfectly pleated slacks, held up by suspenders. Then there was the way he smiled. Even after he stopped talking, Al's subtle smirk from across a room could remind you to not take yourself so seriously—which was ironic, coming from the clean-cut Italian engineer. But that was part of his charm. He could make you sit up straight and fall over laughing in the same moment. Like Lois, he would beam with a light and a love for life that was contagious.

Once, before he got so sick, Al and his wife, Madelyn, invited Ashley and me over for dinner. He told us a story in which he started cracking up and couldn't stop. In turn, we all broke down, laughing hysterically. We never heard the punch line. All I remember is the warmth of that man and moment, and how I miss both dearly.

Maybe a year or so before he died, I visited Al in the nursing home. His health had gotten worse, which made it difficult for Madelyn to take care of him all the time. So he entered a home where he could receive twenty-four-hour care, and she was by his side every day. When Madelyn went on a trip, the church decided to take turns visiting Al, making sure he had a familiar face to see nearly every day. When it was my turn to visit, I forgot to bring my wallet. We ate lunch together, and the waitress told me I could pay the bill later. As we ate, Al told me about the war and how he had just visited the World War II Memorial in Washington, D.C. His speech was rough in parts and honestly, I didn't know how cognitive he was. Was he telling me of things he'd done this year — or decades ago? Despite some of the communication challenges, we still managed to exchange a few words in Spanish.

At the end of the meal, the waitress stopped by our table, asking if we'd like any dessert. As she said this, the woman winked at Al, her hand on her hip. He ordered two scoops of ice cream — one vanilla and one chocolate — to be delivered in the same bowl, using hand gestures to make sure she understood. *Even now*, I thought, *so precise*. He encouraged me to get the same.

"It's *really* good," he said.

"I bet it is," I said. But when the waitress turned to me, order ticket in hand, I passed. She returned a few moments later with Al's bowl of ice cream. I watched as he cut into the cold dessert with a spoon, cleanly slicing a piece of vanilla from the two melded scoops. A dollop of white squeezed out from his lips as he slurped it into his mouth, and immediately he knew something was wrong. Putting down the spoon, he picked up a napkin and wiped his mouth clean. There—better now.

Later, Pastor Ron told me Al had eaten healthy his whole life and was never one for sweets or desserts. However, some of his children, during a visit to the nursing home, had finally won him over and encouraged him to try the ice cream. He loved it. Apparently, he had been ordering it ever since, which was why the waitress winked at him, not one bit surprised by what he would order. Looking back, I wish I would have gotten a bowl.

Years later, I still have the order ticket from that lunch. Falling apart from being carried around in my pocket for so many years, that little green ticket serves as a reminder of a man I once knew and the meal we shared together. As I look back, I realize it's also a reminder to order a bowl of ice cream every chance I get.

A few years ago, right before Thanksgiving, our church held a worship service at an old country chapel just outside of town. We were still fairly new to the church, but this was a longstanding tradition. Every year they'd get together to sing songs and share something they were grateful for. Every year has had its moments, but that year was particularly powerful.

I stood and said a few quick words of "thanks" for family and community and especially the support of my wife. Ashley did the same. But then Lois came forward, standing up from her wheelchair with the breathing tubes in her hand to make sure the oxygen tanks continued to do their job. And with rapt attention, we listened.

She began by thanking God for another year of life, remembering how last year she had been praying to simply make it through Christmas. She was sure that would be her last Christmas, and she had just wanted to enjoy one more time with all her family together. But it wasn't. In fact, she still had a few Christmases left in her after that—but none of us knew that then. She told us life was a gift and that she was grateful for her husband and her family. Then she sat down, and Jim wheeled her back to their seats.

After Lois's monologue, Madelyn walked to the front with Al trailing behind her, aided by a walker. I took a deep breath: this was going to be special. Like Lois, Al had been through a difficult year, and most of us wondered how much longer he'd make it. Listening to his wife speak, he stood by her side, grinning from ear to ear; at that point, he wasn't speaking much, but he never stopped smiling. Madelyn said the same things Lois did—that life was a gift, something to be cherished, a privilege to be appreciated—but she also issued a strong challenge. She said she had no regrets and reminded us to live our lives with the same gusto: to enjoy every hug, relish every tear, and be grateful for every moment. She talked about tragedies and challenges and the overwhelming goodness of God. And then she finished. But before she stepped down from the pulpit area, Madelyn turned to Al, asking with her slight southern twang, "How was that?"

For the first time in a long time, we heard Al speak: "You did great!"

With tears in our eyes, we laughed. Madelyn returned to her seat with her husband, the two of them holding hands.

Mesmerized by the moment, I realized how many opportunities I'd already let slip away. I turned to Ashley. Reaching for her arm, I let my fingers slide all the way from her elbow to her hand; as I felt my fingers wrap around hers, I squeezed. Without looking, she squeezed back. And I knew I would do my best to reach for her hand not just at that moment, but often—as often as I could. I don't know if Al thought that his life turned out the way he'd expected, but I hope he knew that he gave us all a gift that day. And as I turned to listen to Pastor Ron conclude the service, I kept hold of my wife's hand.

That winter, Al's health worsened, and he spent several months in that nursing home I mentioned. For a season, he seemed to get better, and two years later, we heard the news of his passing. We buried him on a hot summer day in July—hotter than the day we buried Lois—and I tried not to cry. But when I heard the preacher who was eulogizing him reference the "greatest generation" to which he belonged, I nodded furiously.

Yes, that was him.

My friend Sue reached over to place her hand on my back, and I cried.

Part of me thought Al and Lois would live forever. They had lived such full lives and already been through so much; what was stopping them from continuing? Certainly not death. I had moved into town at a time when these two were at the end of their lives. Their families and doctors didn't expect them to live as long as they did, and if the odds had been right, I never would have met them at all. But I did. And during that sweet in-between season, what I saw was but a fraction of their story—but it was enough. Enough to know and admire them. And I'm grateful for the time, inspired by it, and better because of it. Because of them.

I wish I would've tapped into the wisdom of these old souls sooner. I wish I would have listened more, visited more, made myself more available. I suppose we all feel this way when someone we know passes—remembering moments when we could have done and been more, but didn't. However, I'm grateful for what I did have, because the slivers of their stories I got to witness taught me that every part in a person's story is important, even the final scenes. For the few years I knew them, Lois and Al weren't biding their time. They weren't waiting to die. They were squeezing every drop of marrow they could out of the moments life had given them, not wasting a single one.

Because of Al and Lois and the scenes I was privileged to witness, I'm inspired to live like I mean it—to make the most of my days, however many or few I have left. I'm still early in my story, still somewhere in between the beginning and the end. Like Al and Lois, I long to live well with whatever time I have left.

I had better get started.

IN-BETWEEN GLIMPSES

I've learned patience as a grandmother. I didn't realize I expected my daughter to get things done quickly and efficiently—fun things, like coloring!— until I became a grandmother. My grandchildren range in age from one to eleven years, and through those eleven years, I've learned to sit while small hands color or young brains figure out game strategy or developing personalities tell me about their friends and school. I've even learned to sit patiently and watch while I'm shown how to play video games (that's the biggest test of my patience!). I will now sit and let a child ramble on without trying to direct the conversation, as I've discovered you hear much more when you listen. These have been great lessons for me, and the skills carry over to the adult parts of my life.

—Kathy

Conclusion

The other week, I read an article in the *Harvard Business Review* about why people don't hate waiting.[11]

Well, this looks interesting, I thought.

Turns out, it's true. People don't hate waiting when they know what they're waiting for. What drives people nuts, though, is the postponements that happen for no apparent reason, the arbitrary delays and setbacks.

We hate waiting for the things we think we deserve now, not later: the spot at the front of the line, hot food from the kitchen, the best job in the company. It's not the waiting we dislike; we understand some things take time. What we loathe is the time after what we deem to be an appropriate amount of waiting. We can all be patient—to an extent—but then we have our limits.

Our problem, then, is not one of impatience, but entitlement.

Life is waiting. Not just waiting in line at the grocery store or waiting to renew your driver's license, but waiting to love and commit and find the work you were meant to do. Our lives are full of inconvenient setbacks, not due to some great cosmic mistake but because of some divine purpose we don't comprehend.

In the waiting, we become.

Recently, I conducted an online survey with some of my readers, asking what they struggled with when it comes to waiting. Most said they were "sometimes" or "often" patient people. For the majority of readers, it was only a certain something that challenged their patience. One person said their waiting period had been a "twenty-seven-year journey." Some individuals shared that they were waiting to find a certain vocation, while others were tired of waiting for traffic lights or for their kids to grow up.

Everyone has something they're waiting for.

But what if waiting was not simply some grand inconvenience, as we often treat it, but rather the very tool God uses to shape and change us? If that were the case, we might have to change how we react to those delays and interruptions. We might have to pause and wonder what lesson we need to learn here, what opportunity we have to find the next piece of our destiny.

By the end of this journey, you would think with all this self-examination that I'd be a little more patient, a little more forgiving at the stoplight. But no. I am just as rude and impatient as ever. Why is this? What's wrong with me? Maybe nothing. Maybe I'm just in process—still becoming, still learning. What I'm waiting for now is not what I waited for when I was twelve or twenty-two. There are always new opportunities to learn to live in the waiting, because the lessons I need are evolving with me. As always, I resist them with every step of the way. Don't we all?

Although we may now recognize that waiting is a tool that helps us grow, that doesn't change the fact that the growth is still uncomfortable, sometimes even painful. Nobody likes to be stretched and pulled, but unfortunately, this is the only way we grow.

Most people understand that in order to get from one place to the next, you must travel; you have to move. But few are willing to accept this in areas of personal growth. We can't stand still; we will stagnate. The irony is that when we think we are standing still, we are actually growing the most. What gets us to our destinations are the pauses, the breaks, the in-between.

So it is with this wonderful experiment we call life. We don't slow down when we should, so we must be stopped. Diverted. Stalled. And these moments—these huge inconveniences, if we can dare call them that anymore—set us aright, reminding us not only of how far we've come but also of the fact that we are not done.

Yet.

Notes

1. Annie Dillard, *The Writing Life* (New York: Harper Perennial, 1990), 32.

2. James Gunn, *Super*, directed by James Gunn (New York: IFC Films, 2010).

3. Francis Charles Whiston, *Teach Us to Pray* (Eugene, OR: Wipf and Stock Publishers, 2009), 152.

4. Jim Adkins and Tom Linton, "Goodbye Sky Harbor," Jimmy Eat World (Los Angeles: Capitol Records, 1999).

5. Martin Davidson and Arlene Davidson, *Eddie and the Cruisers*, directed by Martin Davidson (Los Angeles: Embassy Pictures, 1983).

6. Shauna Niequist, *Cold Tangerines* (Grand Rapids, MI: Zondervan, 2010).

7. Steven Pressfield, "More from Turning Pro," Steven Pressfield Online, June 13, 2012. www.stevenpressfield.com/2012/06/more-from-turning-pro/.

8. Oswald Chambers, "The Consciousness of the Call," *My Utmost for His Highest*, September 29, 2012. http://utmost.org/classic/the-consciousness-of-the-call-classic/.

9. Ben Gibbard and Nick Harmer, "What Sarah Said" (New York: Atlantic Records, 2005).

10. C. S. Lewis, *The Lion, the Witch, and the Wardrobe* (Grand Rapids, MI: Zondervan, 2000), 2.

11. Ryan W. Buell and Michael I. Norton, "Think Customers Hate Waiting? Not So Fast . . ." *Harvard Business Review*, May 2011. http://hbr.org/2011/05/think-customers-hate-waiting-not-so-fast/ar/1.

Acknowledgments

I hate writing this part. It's the hardest, because you don't want to forget anyone. I'm sure I will, though, which is why we should call this section "Apologies" instead of Acknowledgments. Let me say sorry ahead of time.

This book took an army to write (so if it's not any good, blame the army, not me). I am indebted to those who have encouraged, assisted, and inspired me to finish this work, some even unwittingly. So to all of you who made this possible, thank you.

To my wife, Ashley, for her endless patience with my misremembering things. Thanks for holding me accountable to telling the truth, babe. And to my son, Aiden, for being present for the writing of much of this book. Thanks to your early-morning bouncing, laughing, and spitting, I didn't take myself too seriously.

To my family, for giving me the foundation for so many of these stories. Thanks, Mom, for forgiving me for tossing out those earrings and for reading the dictionary to me on road trips. To my dad, for giving me my first guitar and always encouraging me to be creative. To my younger sisters and brother, for your love; I hope I make you guys proud.

To my team of mentors: Mike Hyatt, for his generosity and encouragement; Ken Davis, for teaching me that words matter more than I realize; and to Marion Roach Smith, for telling me when I could do better. Also, to my former boss, Seth Barnes, for being the first to call me a professional writer. Without that affirmation, I never would have started.

To Ann Kroeker, for helping me turn a bunch of chaotic anecdotes into some semblance of a story. And for helping me find more of my voice in the process, thank you.

To my friends who call me out and keep me going: Joe Bunting, Andy Traub, Chad Jarnagin, Dustin Damery, Paul Vasilko, Christine Niles, David Molnar (and the rest of the Young Eagles group), and my Franklin Fellowship family. You guys make me better.

To my teachers and peers who inspire me more than they know: Seth Godin, Jon Acuff, Ian Cron, Shauna Niequist, Madeleine L'Engle, C. S. Lewis, and many others.

To my agent, Mark Oestreicher, who coaxes me off ledges when I need it. To Bailey Utecht, for being the final editor on this book: thank you for bringing order to this chaos. And to Randall Payleitner and the rest of Moody Collective, who see things in me that I'm just beginning to see myself. I am continually encouraged and amazed by all your faith; thank you.

And to Jesus, who saved me and set me apart and constantly teaches me to be present to the moment. I am grateful and honored to pursue this calling You've given me.

And to you, dear reader, for picking up this book and (I hope) reading it. Most people skip this section, so thanks for paying attention.

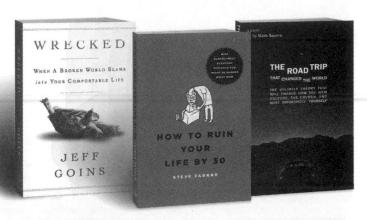

also available as ebooks

moody
collective

Moody Collective brings words of life to a generation seeking deeper faith. We are a part of Moody Publishers, representing this next generation of followers of Christ through books, blogs, essays, and more.

We seek to know, love, and serve the millennial generation with grace and humility. Each of our books is intended to challenge and encourage our readers as they pursue God. To learn more, visit our website, www.moodycollective.com.

WRECKED

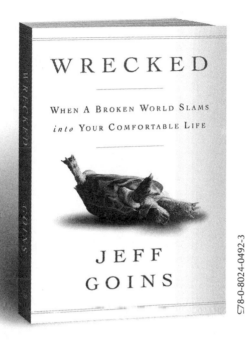

Wrecked is about the life we wish we lived.

It's a life of radical sacrifice and selfless service—and how we find it in the midst of suffering. *Wrecked* is a look at how we discover our life's purpose in the least likely of places: in the tough spots and amongst the broken-hearted. *Wrecked* is a manifesto for living like we mean it; it's a guide to growing up and giving your life away. This book is for us. A generation of young adults pursuing our life's work both responsibly and radically—how to live in the real-world tension of sacrificial living and the daily mundane.

also available as an ebook

MOODY
PUBLISHERS

www.MoodyPublishers.com

How do you pack for all fifty states?

978-0-8024-0729-0

When I was in college, I figured my life would come together around graduation. I'd meet a guy; we'd plan a beautiful wedding and buy a nice house—not necessarily with a picket fence, but with whatever kind of fence we wanted. I might work, or I might not, but whatever we decided, I would be happy.

When I got out of college and my life didn't look like that, I floundered around, trying to figure out how to get the life I had always dreamed of. Just when I had given up all hope of finding the "life I'd always dreamed about," I decided to take a trip to all fifty states...because when you go on a trip, you can't take your baggage. What I found was that "packing light" wasn't as easy as I thought it was.

This is the story of that trip and learning to live life with less baggage.
also available as an ebook

MOODY
PUBLISHERS

www.MoodyPublishers.com

TELL ME A STORY

978-0-8024-0856-3

All the best stories have a few things in common—sometimes, we just have to step back from our daily routine to see them. First, we need the voice of a narrator or a storyteller. Then, add in some interesting characters, throw them into a risky setting, and get ready for a good dose of conflict. Give those characters a purpose or goal and then…well, then the real action begins!

When we recognize the elements of a great story, we begin to see our lives as a part of God's story. Then, we'll better understand what He has for us, what we should believe about this story, and what we should then do.

God's story is happening. We are right in the middle of a page-turner—and God is with us in it. Start seeing your life as a part of God's story and make some great adventures happen right now!

also available as an ebook

MOODY
PUBLISHERS

www.MoodyPublishers.com